Douglas

MacArthur

Young Protector

Illustrated by Gray Morrow

Douglas MacArthur

Young Protector

By Laura Long

THE **BOBBS-MERRILL** COMPANY, INC.
A SUBSIDIARY OF HOWARD W. SAMS & CO., INC.
Publishers • INDIANAPOLIS • NEW YORK

GOSHEN, IND.

LIBRARY OF CONGRESS CATALOG CARD NUMBER: 65-14815

PRINTED IN THE UNITED STATES OF AMERICA

For Lesley Ann Morris
who has recently discovered that
a good book
is one that has something to say
to her mind and heart

Illustrations

Numerous smaller illustrations

Contents

★ ★ ★ ★

Books by Laura Long

DAVID FARRAGUT: BOY MIDSHIPMAN
DOUGLAS MacARTHUR: YOUNG PROTECTOR
GEORGE DEWEY: VERMONT BOY
OLIVER HAZARD PERRY: BOY OF THE SEA

★ # Douglas
MacArthur
Young Protector

The Bird Was
an Arrow

CAPTAIN ARTHUR MACARTHUR and his family
had just finished breakfast when the buckboard
came to take Arthur and Malcolm to school. The
two boys kissed their mother and ran out the
door. Douglas or Dougie, the youngest son,
squirmed off his chair and ran after them. The
captain followed his sons more slowly.

There already were several children in the
buckboard, all on their way to school. "Hurry!"
they called to Arthur and Malcolm.

The two boys raced to the buckboard. "Good
morning!" they said to the corporal, who had
come to take them to school.

11

Arthur was seven years old and Malcolm was only five, not really old enough to attend school. The school was taught by an officer's wife in an old shed on the army post. She had said it was all right for Malcolm to come.

The post was Fort Wingate in New Mexico Territory. Captain MacArthur of the United States Army was the commanding officer at the post. There was a Navaho Indian Reservation a few miles from the post. One of the leading duties of the post was to keep the Indians on the reservation contented and peaceful.

Keeping peace was hard because three government officials had made promises that the government could not keep. The Navahos had made promises and kept them.

Captain MacArthur smiled at the little blond boy who stood outside, wildly waving both arms. The children in the buckboard called wildly to him, "Come with us, Dougie!"

12

"Some day you'll be old enough!"

"How old are you now, Dougie?"

The child looked at his small hand. Slowly he closed his thumb and little finger across his palm. He held up the other three fingers. He was three years old.

Captain MacArthur talked with the corporal who was driving the buckboard. "The Indians are restless, Corporal. Did you hear the drums and the war chants all night?"

"Yes, sir, Captain. I did, sir," answered the corporal. "They've been threatening to burn us out, I have heard."

"The government promised them fifteen thousand sheep, which are hard to obtain. The sheep haven't been delivered, and the weather is turning cold. The Indians soon will need both wool and mutton. Just don't forget to be careful, Corporal. Remember to keep your eyes in the back of your head as well as in front."

The corporal grinned. "I'll do that, sir," he said. He clucked to his team, and the wheels of the buckboard began to turn.

The captain picked up his youngest son to carry him back to the house. "Who taught you how to say you are three years old?" he asked.

"Arthur," said Dougie. Once more he folded his thumb and little finger inside his palm. His three extended fingers looked very big to him. He must really be growing up.

"The next time anyone asks you when you were born, Dougie," he said, "tell them January 26, 1880. Do you know where you were born or where your brothers were born?"

"You were born at Little Rock, Arkansas, and your brothers were born at my father's house in Norfolk, Virginia," Mrs. MacArthur said.

"Your mother's family settled in Virginia, but my family settled in Wisconsin," the captain explained to the young listener.

"We had planned for you to be born at my father's house in Virginia," Mrs. MacArthur said. "You would have been, too, but you came a little earlier than we expected."

"Yes, I still remember the announcement in the Norfolk newspaper. It read, 'A son was born to Captain and Mrs. Arthur MacArthur, while his parents were away from home.'"

"Finish your oatmeal, Dougie," said his mother, after his father started to leave.

The captain went as far as the door, then came back. He took a drink of coffee from his wife's cup and stood leaning over her.

"There might be a raid today," he said. "Maybe you should take Dougie and go to the schoolhouse. Then you and the children would be together and could help one another."

"Will you be there too?" she asked. "I want to be where you are."

"You can't be, because I have work to do."

15

"Yes, I know that you have, and very serious work, too." She patted his chin.

When Captain MacArthur left, Mrs. MacArthur smiled at her small son, but he could see a little wrinkle between her eyes. He knew she was worried about something.

"Now get to work on your oatmeal," she said.

This was the time of day Dougie loved best of all. His father and older brothers were gone for the day and he and his mother were at home alone. He had no intention of hurrying with his oatmeal. He knew that as soon as he finished eating, his mother would start her day's work, and he would be left to entertain himself. He had just taken a mouthful of oatmeal when Sergeant Ripley entered through the kitchen.

"Mrs. MacArthur, the captain sent me to bring you and the boy to the schoolhouse. We have a mite of a war going on with the Navahos. You'll have to hurry a bit to make it."

16

Dougie noticed a strange light in his mother's eyes, as she lifted him swiftly from his chair. She forgot his oatmeal. The big dictionary on which he sat slipped to the floor, but nobody bothered to pick it up.

"Very good, Sergeant," said Mrs. MacArthur, holding her head high. "Start marching."

"Give me the boy, ma'am," said the sergeant. "He's a load to carry uphill."

"No. He'll be safer with me in a woman's clothing. We'll make a papoose out of him."

She fastened her long wool scarf about Dougie's waist and drew the ends over her shoulders and about her waist to make a harness. She felt behind her for Dougie's ankles and tied them about her. Dougie leaned against her back and sighed with relief. He knew that she would not let anything hurt him.

Mrs. MacArthur and the sergeant ran as fast as they could, up the long, steep hill to the schoolhouse. Dougie, looking backwards, could see three Indians with painted faces, wearing feathers in their black hair. The Indians dodged from one cactus bush to another.

He saw one Indian lift his arms and heard him give a horrible cry. At the same instant he saw a brightly colored bird coming from the Indian toward him. The boy lifted his arms to seize the bird, but it went too fast.

His mother grabbed his arm and screamed. This frightened him, and he hid his head on her shoulder and began to cry.

"My bird! My pretty bird!" he sobbed. "Why did it get away?"

"Lucky it did!" cried his mother. "That was an Indian arrow. Six inches to the right, and it would have killed you."

"Close shave," said the sergeant, "but it missed us. Better give me the boy, ma'am. You're not as steady as when we started."

18

They waited for Mrs. MacArthur to get her breath. The sergeant pulled the arrow from the sand. It was buried almost to its top feather. It had hit the ground with great force.

The sergeant smiled as he looked at the arrow. "The Navaho who made this was better at making arrows pretty than he was at making them accurate. This one has too many feathers."

Mrs. MacArthur could not stop trembling. "Sergeant, we must take time to thank God for saving us," she said.

The sergeant was reluctant. "Make it quick, ma'am. Just say, 'God, we thank You because the Navaho had poorly made arrows.'"

Mary MacArthur smiled and shook a lock of hair from her cheek. "That does very nicely, Sergeant. Shall we start marching?"

At the schoolhouse Dougie let the children examine his arrow. They agreed with him that it looked like a bird.

Mrs. MacArthur told the children what had happened. Then she explained what they needed to do for protection during the rest of the day. They were to stay in the schoolhouse until the last Indian had been driven off the post. Then the buckboard would come for them.

The buckboard came earlier than usual. The corporal had orders to get everyone home before dark. The Indians might come back after dark. Then they would be hard to see.

Mrs. MacArthur was afraid that the Indian scare might upset young Dougie. She didn't want him to feel that he should always be afraid of Indians. He must not be afraid of anyone or anything in the world. She must train him to be as brave as his father.

She sat down in a low chair in her bedroom and took Dougie on her lap. She stroked his hair and felt thankful because he was safe. Somehow she felt that The Lord had saved him, just as He had saved the baby Moses in the Bible. She felt very close to The Lord at that moment.

"About what happened today, Dougie," she began. Dougie thought from the tone of her voice that she was about to tell him a Bible story. She had a special voice for Bible stories. But instead, she told him about the arrow.

"Now you see how God can save persons He wants to save," she told him. "You don't ever need to feel afraid. No matter where you are, or in what kind of danger, God will be there, too. He can save you better than you ever can save yourself. I'm sure He saved you from that arrow today because He has work that He wants you to do after you become a man. He wants you to be as brave as your father."

Dougie listened without really knowing what his mother was saying. Most of all he liked the way she held him close and the way she spoke in a gentle voice. It gave him a comfortable feeling to hear her say that God was interested in seeing him grow into a man as brave as his father. He loved his father and often watched him and imitated the things that his father did.

Sadness in the Family

THE SUN SHONE almost too brightly. It was spring, though the snow on the distant mountains still gave off brilliant colors at sunset. The children on the post found their books tiresome. The officer's wife, too, wanted to quit teaching, because it was time for making a garden and cleaning house. School, therefore, was dismissed for the summer.

Dougie was happy to have his brothers home. Now he often shared their adventures. Arthur, who had a pony of his own, let Dougie ride with him. Malcolm, a quiet boy, taught his small brother how to play jackstraws.

23

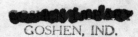

Visitors—explorers, traders, gold hunters, railroad men—began to come to the camp. Some of them brought their families. The captain thought that New Mexico would soon have more than enough colonists to become a state.

"Why shouldn't it?" he said. "Where else can you find a land with such gorgeous coloring as New Mexico?"

"And so little water," added his wife. "Where else can boys find so many good reasons for never washing their hands? Boys, please wash your hands for supper—but don't all of you wash at once. Don't waste any water."

Every day a soldier drove an army cart to the Puereos River, where dozens of barrels were filled with water for the people on the post. Sometimes the water was yellow or reddish-gold—pretty to see, but not good to use. Mrs. MacArthur was always careful to boil every drop of water before she allowed anyone to drink it.

Sometimes the soldiers came back with the barrels still empty, because there was no water in the river. One day Sergeant Ripley let the boys go with him for water.

Malcolm looked at Dougie. "You don't mean him, too, do you, Sergeant?"

"Yes, why not?" said the sergeant.

Dougie made it quite clear that he wanted to go. He tossed his hat in the air and let out a scream louder than a Navaho chant.

The sergeant stopped the cart at the spot where the winter snow had left the river the deepest. The older boys jumped down to help roll off the barrels. But before Dougie could jump, Sergeant Ripley was holding him by the shoulder.

"Look, Dougie, I'm in charge here. Every man must do what I tell him, and I tell you to stay on this wagon. Military orders. Obey!"

Dougie obeyed.

While the soldiers were filling the barrels with water, an Indian squaw came to the bank of the river. Like most of the Navaho women, she was dressed in bright colors, which looked very pretty in the sun. On her back she carried a roll of bright-colored blankets.

The squaw and her family had spent the winter weaving the blankets, and now she wanted to sell them. She spread them on the ground for the soldiers to see. Arthur and Malcolm each picked up a blanket and wrapped himself in it. But they had no money to buy one.

The boys did not help to load the heavy barrels on the cart. Four men, two on the ground and two on the cart, lifted each barrel from the ground. As the boys watched the men work, they talked about the beautiful blankets and wished their mother had come with them.

"She would have bought one," Arthur declared. "I know she would, for they are pretty."

"I'd like to have one," said Malcolm, "for when I am sick in bed."

Arthur laughed. "When would that be? Have you ever been sick in bed?"

"No, but I might be some day."

That day was to come all too soon. Less than a week later, both Arthur and Malcolm had sniffles and then a cough. Their eyes turned red, and they broke out with red dots. They had the measles. A few days later, Dougie broke out in the same way. By that time, half the camp had the measles.

Arthur recovered from the measles before Dougie took them. He insisted that he had given his speckles to Dougie.

Instead of getting better, Malcolm seemed to get worse. He coughed more. He wheezed more. He could not get his breath. The doctor shook his head sadly. "This is pneumonia," he said. "I can do nothing."

The captain, his wife, and the doctor sat hour after hour by Malcolm's bedside, watching for him to pass through the turning point of pneumonia. If he lived through the night, he would get well. If not——

His mother fainted when the doctor told her that he was dead. Magdelena, the Mexican housekeeper, screamed and prayed, "Mia Maria! Mia Maria! Salve! Salve!" It was a sad, sad household. Dougie walked about the house on his tiptoes. Even Arthur would not smile.

The captain told the boys that their mother wanted to take Malcolm back to Virginia to bury him with her own people.

"We'll move to another camp before long," said the captain. "We can't leave Malcolm here alone. Magdelena will take good care of you, but you must obey her. We won't be gone long. Thank God there's a railroad that will take us all the way to Virginia and back quickly."

28

"I miss you already," said Dougie, "but I miss Mamma the most."

Magdelena, who shared the joys and sorrows of the family, did what she could to bring back good cheer in the house. She gradually hid Malcolm's books and toys from the boys. She kept her own spirits high and sang lively songs. She often asked Sergeant Ripley to take the boys with him on the water cart.

"When your mamma is home again, do not expect her always to be gay and loving," she warned them. "There will be times when she may not seem to see you, but this will not mean that she does not love you. It will only mean that she is still sad about little Malcolm."

When the MacArthurs came home, Magdelena saw that her warning was not needed. There would be no cloud of gloom over the boys. The captain held out his arms and lifted each of his sons high. Mrs. MacArthur grabbed

them and held them tightly. She laughed and
kissed them and told them how glad she was to
be back.

Malcolm's death seemed to bring the family
closer together. The captain spoke to his wife
with a new tenderness. "Pinky," he called her,
"my beautiful Pinky." She, in turn, spoke to her
children with a new tenderness, as if she loved
them more than she ever had before.

Magdelena finally found the courage to men-
tion the changed feelings. "Senora mia," she
said, "I have felt fear that you might still be held
by your grief, but it is not so?"

"Of course I grieve, Magdelena, but God has
been very good to me. I still have two fine sons.
Now I'm adding my love for Malcolm to my love
for Arthur and Dougie."

Magdelena nodded. Malcolm seemed to have
left this extra gift for his brothers.

"Buena," said Magdelena.

The Hot, Dry Desert

BEFORE LONG CAPTAIN MACARTHUR asked for a change of station. He wanted to get the members of his family away from Fort Wingate, where everything reminded them of Malcolm. Finally he received orders, telling him to take his company to Fort Selden, many miles away.

The troops were to march from Fort Wingate, in northwestern New Mexico Territory, to a place on the Rio Grande River, about fifty miles north of El Paso, Texas. First they would follow a Navaho Indian trail across the desert. Then they would follow a trail along the Rio Grande to the border of Mexico.

31

The MacArthur boys listened happily to the talk about being sent to Fort Selden. They heard exciting stories about a Mexican Indian outlaw, named Geronimo. The American army had captured Geronimo several times, but he had always managed to escape. At present he and a band of thieves were stealing cattle and horses all over New Mexico and Arizona.

When Geronimo had escaped from the army, he had gone to Mexico. There he had gathered about him all the bandits and thieves he could find. Now he and his band were growing bolder and bolder in their raids.

Whenever the army tried to capture Geronimo and his band, they would hurry back to Mexico where the army could not follow them. MacArthur's company was being sent to Fort Selden to keep them from crossing the Rio Grande.

The company left Fort Wingate in New Mexico early one morning in July. It was a much smaller company than most companies in the army. The travelers included the MacArthur family, a lieutenant and his family, a company doctor and his family, and forty-seven men.

The men marched, and the women and children rode in two covered wagons, one of which also served as an ambulance. There were two battle wagons and a flock of pack mules. The supplies were firmly strapped to the mules.

Arthur and Dougie often marched with Sergeant Ripley at the head of the column, trying to match their short steps with his long strides. At first Dougie thought this was great fun, but his feet soon grew tired and the hot sun beat upon him until he was glad to go back to the shade of the wagon. The road led across a desert, between and over mountains. The new camp was three hundred miles away.

The men were hot and thirsty, but no matter how thirsty they were at every stop, they could have only a small cup of water. They could not risk running out of water on the desert.

One day Sergeant Ripley pointed out something in the distance that looked like a ridge of brown stone. "See that?" he asked.

"What is it?" asked Arthur.

"A Zuni village or pueblo. See the corn growing and the sheep grazing nearby? The Zuni Indians live in pueblos, like that. The Navahos live in houses made of stone and mud. The Apaches live in wickiups."

While he was talking, half a dozen Indians rode up to the caravan on their horses. They asked to talk to the leader.

The Indians showed by their actions that they were friendly. They wanted to help the travelers in any way that they could on the hot, dry desert country. They even invited the captain and his family and a few others to stay in their village instead of in camp.

With a quick glance at his wife, the captain accepted. Dougie could tell that his mother was surprised, but she seldom objected to anything her husband decided to do.

The boys were delighted. The Indian chief led them to one of the adobe houses in the pueblo. They were to sleep there, but they would eat with the Indians in their estufa, which was the family room of the village. The estufa was a very large, round room with a bright fire burning in the center.

The men and boys sat on the floor, but a polite young Zuni brought three-legged stools for the white women to use. The Indian women kept busy, serving food on large trays. They moved swiftly through the crowd, being careful not to step on anyone's feet.

The trays were loaded with loaves of corn bread, hot corn dodgers, and paper-thin pancakes, crisp and hot, called bunjabes. Other trays were piled high with slices of watermelon and muskmelon, peaches and apricots, separated by rows of toasted pine nuts.

When the group finished eating, the chief told the captain that the young men would entertain them with a mock battle. The warriors chose sides, like children playing a game. The two sides faced each other. Suddenly they started screaming at one another, flashing spears through the air, and firing old-fashioned muskets. Above all the noise, the women kept beating drums and urging their men to victory.

The noise startled Dougie, and he looked about the huge room for his mother. Before long he saw her laughing and knew that everything was being done in fun.

After a short time he joined his father to watch the warriors. Soon he leaned his head against his father's knees and went to sleep.

The visitors were surprised to find magpies,

hawks, and other wild birds flying about the estufa and roosting wherever they could find a place. When the noisy mock battle started, the magpies, hawks, and a lonely goose added their share to the pandemonium. While Dougie was sleeping, a bright-colored oriole, wakened from its sleep, rubbed its beak on his head and sun-tanned cheeks.

At last the oriole caused Dougie to wake up. He sat up straight on the floor, wondering where he was and what had happened. At first he thought he was back at Fort Wingate where the sound of the train whistle had often wakened him in the night. Surely this was the noise which had caused him to awaken.

"What time is it?" he asked sleepily. "Was that the train going through?"

His father and the men about him laughed. They tried to tell him what had happened, but he wouldn't believe them. Even when they showed him the oriole that had wakened him, he thought they were only teasing him.

The captain and his troops started on their way early the next morning. They **couldn't** travel very far each day, because the hot sand of the desert burned their feet. The boys had learned not to ask for a drink when they were thirsty. They had to wait until the road ahead seemed to be floating in the bright sunshine.

One day Dougie became so hot from the heat of the desert, that he couldn't keep going. When his mother saw his flushed face, she knew that he should have water.

"Maybe I could spare half a cup or so," the captain decided. "The men can't go without water when they are marching. Keep Dougie with you in the wagon. I'll bring his cup."

Just then the Indian interpreter beckoned to the captain and to Dougie. He stopped by the roadside and began to dig in the soft sand. He

dug deeper and deeper. Soon he looked up at them with twinkling eyes.

"Good!" he cried. "Good!"

As the interpreter spoke, silvery water sprang from the earth like a fountain. The Indian showed the boys how to bend over it to drink. The men who were close by shouted. Soon the men were drinking and filling the water vessels.

Mrs. MacArthur was sure that the water was a blessing from God. She felt again that God was intervening to protect her sons.

"How did you know there was an underground spring at this particular spot?" she asked.

"The water, she speak to me through this stick that I carry." The Indian held up a wooden pole that he used as a staff.

The animals had to have water as well as the people who were traveling. Once the soldiers stopped a man on a mule to ask him the distance to the next water hole.

"About ten miles," the man answered.

The men marched on for three more hours and stopped another traveler. "How far to the next water?" they called.

"About ten miles," the man told them.

Sergeant Ripley had a ready comment when the troops groaned. "Men, that's good news. Now we know that we aren't marching backwards. Let's get to that water."

Although the soldiers grumbled, they knew that it did very little good. Water could be found only at certain spots in the desert. In some places it could be obtained only by digging in the sand to uncover a spring. In other places it overflowed and stood in pools nearby. The animals especially liked to drink from the pools.

Usually the men tried to pick camping places near spots where there was water. Sometimes, however, the water had a bitter taste or a dark color from chemicals in the ground.

The desert had its own special kinds of plants. There were cactus plants of many sizes and shapes, some with brilliant flowers. There were scattered scraggly pines on the slopes and a few cottonwoods in the valleys. Yet from the few trees and sparse undergrowth, the men always managed to build campfires.

The nights on the desert were very cool. Usually the boys rolled themselves in their blankets and sat near the bright fire. They watched the stately mountains, which had been brightly colored in the sunshine, turn gray and then deep blue. Half asleep, they heard the men discuss Geronimo and how he could be captured. Sometimes they argued how battles had been won or lost in the War between the States.

By this time Dougie usually was asleep.

Learning and Growing

On clear sunny days, the troops could travel only about ten miles. On cloudy days they sometimes traveled eighteen miles, but there were not many cloudy days. In the mountains, they traveled more slowly.

"We're marching forever," complained Dougie. "Why don't we get there?"

"Because we've come only about half way," explained his mother. "Three hundred miles is three hundred miles."

At the next rest stop Dougie climbed down from the wagon to walk beside Sergeant Ripley. He noticed that the scenery was beginning to look different. There were more pine trees. The desert flowers were in full bloom. The mountains in the distance were no longer blue, but of many different colors. Sometimes they rose almost straight up in the air.

"Yell," said Sergeant Ripley.

Douglas wondered what he meant.

"Go ahead. Call out your name as loud as you can. Call out your name."

Dougie lifted his chin and called out his name as loud as he could. Then the sound came back, long-drawn-out—"Doug—las MacAr—thur!" Again he called and the sound came back long-drawn-out. "Douggg— Arrr——thirrr!"

"What makes the sound come back like that?" he asked. He was quite sure that Sergeant Ripley knew everything worth knowing.

"That's an echo," said the sergeant. "The sound hits both sides of the cavern and makes it sound double. Call your name again."

Dougie kept on calling his name until his brother stopped him. "Oh, shut up," said Arthur. "Who wants to listen to that?"

Dougie stopped calling, but the marching feet of the men and the squeak of the wagon wheels sounded double. Without these sounds, there wouldn't have been anything to hear.

"I'm glad I'm not here all by myself," said Arthur. "It would be much too quiet."

Even though there were more trees and other plants now than before, water was still scarce. Most of the streams at this time of the year were completely dry.

One morning two men climbed to the top of a small butte, a flat-topped hill that seemed to grow out of the ground.

"The river! The Rio Grande!" they called from the top. "It's so close we can be there by nightfall!" They had not realized they were so near, because the mountains had cut off the view.

The troops did not waste time in rejoicing. They were eager to start the day's march, so that they could reach the Rio Grande by nightfall. They were no longer afraid of dying of thirst. They could get water now.

They were still a long way from Fort Selden and everyone was tired. More than three weeks had passed since the company had left Fort Wingate in New Mexico.

Fort Selden was a small fort, built chiefly to protect nearby settlers from Indian raids. For many years the Apache Indians had killed and robbed many people who had come here to live. At one time they were doing so much damage to settlers that United States officials offered to pay a bounty for every Apache scalp brought to their stations.

This attempt to control the Apache Nation did little good. The Indians looked upon this action as a step to wiping out their nation. They were proud of their nation and didn't want it destroyed. In recent months they had been causing more trouble than ever before.

When the company reached Fort Selden, the men first looked after the animals. Then Captain MacArthur ordered them to meet on the plaza, or parade ground, in the middle of the post. It was time for retreat.

The company bugler put his heart and soul into his bugle calls for the first evening retreat. The men stood erect and looked at the flag at the top of the flagstaff. They gave out a deep sigh like an evening breeze and some of them shed tears. It was good to be here.

The ceremony started with a speech by the captain, praising the weary soldiers for their courage and patience on the long journey. He explained that parts of the road they had traveled had been trod by explorers and traders for hundreds of years. He also reminded them that they owed thanks to God for His helpful care in crossing the desert and mountains.

During the ceremony Dougie stood very straight and tall. His eyes did not leave the stars and stripes on the flagstaff. Many weeks had passed since he had last stood on a parade ground. Retreat was one of the ceremonies he liked best about army life.

Fort Selden had pretty, one-story houses, which were built of stone and adobe. Captain MacArthur chose a large house in the center of the group. This house was both cool in summer and warm in winter.

Soon the days settled into a regular routine of duties and chores. Every morning Mrs. MacArthur held school for her sons, because there was no regular school at the fort. She taught them how to read and write and to do simple sums. She enjoyed teaching them, but regretted that they couldn't attend a real school.

The boys learned many things outside of school as well as in school. They learned how to ride and to shoot. They even learned how to shoot while they were riding. They learned how to take good care of a horse and how to stay on a mule's back, even when the mule was bucking. There were many horses and mules here.

All kinds of travelers came to Fort Selden. Cowboys taking cattle to El Paso came to request soldier escorts. Railroad men, looking for new routes to the West Coast, frequently stopped. Friendly Indians set up their tents on the parade ground and built their campfires behind the adobe houses.

The boys often accompanied the soldiers who brought water to the fort. They held the horses while the men filled the water barrels. On the way to the river, they passed a butte, or flat-topped hill. On top of this butte there was a heliograph mounted on a tripod.

An army officer formerly stationed at Fort Selden had placed the heliograph on the butte. He had used the instrument to send messages, but now it was no longer needed.

"We have the telegraph now," Sergeant Ripley explained. "We don't need the heliograph."

The ideas of signaling by means of a mirror interested the MacArthur boys and their friend, Will Hughes. One day the three boys asked for picnic lunches to take on a trip to the butte. They wanted to find out, if they could, how the heliograph worked.

First the boys ate their lunches, then started their experiment. They hadn't the least idea how the glass operated, but Arthur, who was the oldest, started to investigate. In a little while he found out how to unlock the instrument and to set it in motion. Then the boys took turns playing with it nearly all afternoon until it was time to go home for supper.

When the boys reached home, they found a number of military tents pitched on the parade ground and a number of horses tied to hitching posts. One of the horses belonged to an officer from Fort Bliss, whom the boys knew. Much to their surprise, the boys received a cool reception inside the MacArthur house.

"Boys," said the captain, "a strange thing happened to Major Smith today. Doubtless you will be able to explain it."

The boys knew that for some reason they were in trouble, but they couldn't tell why. They waited for more information.

"Major Smith and some of his men were on their way to the Apache reservation below here. They had been hearing rumors that Geronimo was in the neighborhood. Suddenly they saw a beam of light coming straight toward them. Major Smith remembered the old heliograph and thought we must be sending him a message."

52

The captain looked straight at his sons. "The beams from the glass were broken and followed no particular pattern," he went on. "They jumped around so that Major Smith decided we were under attack and too excited to know how to use the glass properly. He has brought his troops here to see what was wrong. Now maybe you can explain what the messages meant."

"I'm sorry, but I don't know," said Arthur. "I didn't know there were any messages."

"Arthur played with the glass," put in Dougie, eager to clear himself of all blame. "I told him to leave it alone, but he wouldn't listen to me. He went ahead anyway."

Just then the boys' mother came into the room. She arrived just in time to hear them avoid answering their father.

"Boys," she said, "go wash your faces and hands." She followed them to their bedroom. Then she made them stand and look at her.

"I'm about to ask you a question," she said, "and I expect a true answer. You are going to be punished, but if you tell me a lie, you will be punished doubly. There is no place for a liar in this family. Did either one of you play with the heliograph?"

Dougie started to blame his brother once more for the trouble, but his mother interrupted him and looked at him coldly.

"The thing I hate most, next to a liar, is a tattle-tale," she said. "Let your brother speak for himself, and unless you, too, are guilty, keep your mouth closed."

Dougie kept very still during the rest of the evening. He was proud of Arthur for telling their mother the whole story. He was not sure he would have been so brave.

The boys' punishment followed. They had to stay at home the next day when their parents went on a trip to Las Cruces.

From Station
to Station

WHEN LIFE BECAME monotonous on frontier stations, officers and men went on leave. The captain and his wife went to Las Cruces for a short holiday. News had come that the captain would soon become Major MacArthur, and this was something to celebrate.

Captain MacArthur brought back good news to the soldiers at Fort Selden. He called his men together and told them that at last Geronimo had been captured.

"He'll not get away again this time," the captain told them, but some of the men were doubtful. Geronimo had been captured before, time and again, and he had always escaped. Why wouldn't he escape again?

"Because his captors will not allow him to escape," Captain MacArthur explained. "He will be shot dead if he tries to get away."

The men hoped that this was true. If Geronimo escaped he was certain to stir up trouble with the Apaches.

Shortly after MacArthur became Major MacArthur, he received orders to move to Fort Leavenworth, Kansas. This time Mrs. MacArthur and her two boys went by train.

"We're going in the wrong direction," Dougie complained. "I don't want to go East. I'd rather go to San Francisco."

"Sometime you may get there," said his mother. "People in the army cover the country." She had lived for short periods of time in Little Rock Barracks, Fort Wingate, and Fort Selden. Now she was on her way to live at Fort Leavenworth, a station in Kansas. An army child measures his years by the number of stations that he has called home.

The MacArthurs missed Fort Selden. They missed the mountains and the broad stretches of sandy land, the color and mystery of the desert. They missed the cool, high-ceilinged rooms of their adobe house. Their two-story frame house looked hot and ugly under the Kansas sun.

There were more people at Fort Leavenworth. The MacArthurs would have more friends. There would be more dances and parties, and the children could go to a regular school.

Dougie cared very little for the school. He had never sat in a regular schoolroom before and found it very boring. He hated to do the same things over and over and over.

Outside of school Dougie still practiced shooting with his gun, but he soon found that this was not a popular sport for boys at Fort Leavenworth. The mothers of other children complained because they thought the gun was dangerous. Mrs. MacArthur tried to explain that he had been taught to use the gun carefully.

Another sport that Dougie enjoyed was riding his pony through the country near Fort Leavenworth. One night he dreamed that while he was riding he captured Geronimo.

The officers at Fort Leavenworth had heard much about Geronimo and asked Major MacArthur about him. They wondered how he caused so much trouble with a few men.

"In spite of the rascal's sins—and they are many—we are forced to admit that Geronimo is a successful leader," the major explained to the company. "He never risks his men in places from which they can't escape. He strikes and disappears—a good method of fighting an enemy stronger than you are. Look at the men we have lost trying to catch him, and the Mexicans have lost even more. Geronimo has lost only five men in that many years."

"How does he do it?" asked a lieutenant.

Dougie saw his father smile. "That's what I mean to find out, if I can. It's important to know how to save your own men."

The MacArthurs lived at Fort Leavenworth only a short time. One day the major received word that he was to be transferred to the army headquarters in Washington, D. C. This was a great change, because he no longer would have an opportunity to be with troops.

Dougie and Arthur were greatly disappointed about having to leave the soldiers, especially Sergeant Ripley. Neither boy realized, however, how much he had taught them nor how much this knowledge would mean to them later.

Mrs. MacArthur was delighted with the new assignment in Washington, partly because it was an advancement for her husband, but also because she could be closer to Norfolk, Virginia. Now she could see her relatives again after having been away from them for a long time.

Dougie did not share her pleasure. He disliked everything about life in Washington. Only an Indian child could have known less about cities than he did.

The children at the Force Public School seemed as strange to him as he must have seemed to them. There was no common ground on which he could start to build friendships. Worst of all, he had no pony to ride. The life he had known and loved in the West would not fit into the way he had to live in Washington, D. C.

The MacArthurs lived in Washington longer than they had lived anywhere before. Dougie completed his elementary school work at Force School. Through the years, he learned to like many of his schoolmates, but he greatly missed doing some of the things he had done before.

Two important things happened while the MacArthurs lived in Washington. Arthur received an appointment to the Naval Academy at Annapolis. His father was granted the Medal of Honor, the highest honor given to any military man, officer or soldier. President William H. McKinley presented the medal, only a few months before he was assassinated.

Dougie looked for a long time at the golden star with the word VALOR printed above it. Would he—could he ever be as great a man as his father? Would he ever be as great a man as Arthur would be someday?

When Dougie was thirteen the family moved again——this time to Fort Sam Houston in Texas. All the MacArthurs were happy about moving, because this fort was the largest and most important post in the country.

In Texas Dougie entered the West Texas Military Academy at San Antonio. Here he began to prepare for West Point. Boys who attended good military schools found it easier to pass the entrance examinations at West Point. They were taught what to study and how to study to get along well in answering the questions.

Arthur had passed his examinations at Annapolis without going to a prep school. He had always liked school and didn't need special work. Dougie had never liked school so well.

At West Texas Dougie discovered the importance of study and began to apply himself as never before. He wanted to enter West Point more than he had ever wanted to do anything in his life. The only way he could get into this great military academy was by studying.

When Dougie found how much information could be found between the covers of a book, he read as though he had just stumbled onto a very great treasure. For the first time in his life he stood first in his class.

Every year Dougie spent at West Texas, he played football in the fall and baseball in the spring. He began to get medals for excellence in mathematics, history, and military bearing.

He got medals for football, baseball, and long distance running. He had never been happier.

Then, just six months before he was to graduate, his father, now a lieutenant colonel, was ordered to the Department of the Dakotas, which was Indian country. He would be stationed at St. Paul, Minnesota.

Dougie found it very difficult to think of leaving West Texas Military Academy. Every year he had been first in his class. He had become a tennis champion. He had played quarterback on the football team. He had played shortstop on the baseball team, and now he was manager of the baseball team.

He found it hard to turn his back on these activities. At West Texas he was happier than he had ever been in his life. Perhaps he would never find a school that he liked so well.

Dougie's parents tried to explain that when you serve in the army, you serve your country first, not yourself. You go wherever your commanding officers think you can serve your country best. The orders must be obeyed.

While Colonel MacArthur and his family were getting ready to move, he received a letter from a friend who was a congressman from Wisconsin. If Dougie would like to go to West Point, there would be an opening in the fall of 1899. In order to qualify, he would have to pass the entrance examination in the spring of 1898. This was only a little more than a year away.

"He still needs schooling," said the colonel. "Maybe we should leave him at West Texas."

Mrs. MacArthur was not willing. "Suppose he should get sick, with his parents half way across the country," she said.

"We may go to war with Spain any minute," the colonel said thoughtfully. "If that happens, I'll need to go to the West Indies. Perhaps the best thing is for you to take Dougie to Milwau-

. Then he will be living in the congressman's district when he receives the appointment to West Point. He can continue his studies in Milwaukee as well as here."

"When Dougie goes to West Point, I'll go with him. I'll live on the post, where I can be of some help to him."

So it was decided. In family conferences, Dougie was not asked for his opinion. His parents were his commanding officers. He did what they told him, for he trusted them completely. All he had to do was obey.

Changing from one senior class to another was not easy. The Milwaukee High School seniors had studied subjects that were not taught at West Texas. Also he had studied subjects at West Texas that were not taught at Milwaukee. Besides going ahead with his work at the high school, he needed to continue the subjects that he would be using at West Point. His mother taught him these subjects. Altogether his work was much like taking work in two schools at once but somehow he managed.

When the day for the West Point examination came, Dougie was frightened. He was afraid he might not get good enough grades. He wanted to pass so badly that he didn't know what he would do, if he failed.

He came downstairs, dressed in his best suit. He had shined his shoes as though he planned to use them for mirrors. He sat down to eat breakfast, but the odors of the bacon and toast made him feel sick.

"Eat, Dougie! You'll need energy," said his mother. He shook his head weakly.

"You'll never be able to take that exam on an empty stomach," his mother argued. Dougie agreed, but he had no desire for food. Finally, he took a few bites of oatmeal and tried a slice of crisp bacon. The food made him so sick that he jumped up and ran out of the house. After a few minutes in the fresh air, he began to feel better. Then he went inside again.

His mother's eyes gleamed and he knew that she would have something important to say. "Dougie, you can't let yourself act like this," she said. "You must believe in yourself. You must tell yourself that you know you can pass this examination. Why shouldn't you? You've worked hard, especially this last year."

She looked him in the eye. "Surely you don't want all your work to be wasted. You can't go to this examination—or any other—with the feeling that you're going to fail. Now take a deep breath, and say 'I know that I can pass it,' while you drink your coffee. Then hurry along and do your very best!"

Dougie pulled his mother to him and kissed her. "Thanks, Pinky," he said. He had used his father's pet name for her for the first time.

Now he was all right again. His mother had faith in him, and she nearly always was right. Her faith seemed contagious. He was sorry to have behaved so badly at breakfast.

He found the examination easier than he had expected following his years of preparation. He even had time to look about and to watch others taking the examination. One was tapping his pencil against the desk. Another was frowning, his lips moving in silence.

Douglas was very thankful as he wondered which questions were giving them trouble. If they had gone to West Texas Military Academy or had had mothers like Pinky MacArthur, they wouldn't be having so much trouble.

A week later the congressman telegraphed that Douglas had won the appointment. He had won it with the highest grade ever made by any applicant in the history of the academy. Now he wondered why he had been so upset.

Training at West Point

As young MacArthur grew up, people more and more began to call him Douglas. The only person who called him Dougie was his mother. His father usually called him Doug.

After Douglas received his grades from West Point, he was ordered to have a complete physical examination. At first the army doctor who examined him could find nothing wrong with him.

At last the doctor motioned for Douglas to lie on a table. "I want to pound on your spine a little," he explained.

Douglas, in his long underwear, lay flat on his stomach, so that the doctor could examine his back. Suddenly he felt a pain so intense that he screamed.

"Ow!" he cried. "What caused that?"

"Let's find out," said the doctor, prodding deeper along Douglas' backbone. He gave a sudden twist to the bone, and Douglas began to shake. The pain was so sharp that he went black for a minute. When he came to, the pain was slowly passing away.

"What happened?" he asked, still twitching a little from pain.

"You have a pinched nerve," replied the doctor. "You can't get into West Point with that kind of nerve in your back."

This report from the doctor was hard for Douglas to believe. "I have to go to West Point," he said pleadingly. "I have the appointment. I've passed the exams."

"Not your physical," replied the doctor. "I can't let you enter West Point with a back like that. You couldn't possibly stand the first year of training there."

"What—is there anything I can do?"

"Maybe. You can try, anyway. First, you need an operation to free that pinched nerve. Then you need exercise and still more exercise. You've taught yourself to move so that the nerve doesn't bother you, but it's made all the muscles in your back tense."

As Douglas left the doctor's office, he tried to plan how to tell his mother. His father, now Major General MacArthur, had left for the Philippines only a few days before. His brother Arthur, too, was on his way to the Philippines with the Navy. His mother had enough problems without his adding to them.

As he neared home, he felt better about telling his mother. He felt that somehow she would know what to do and would give him sound advice. Through the years he had come to have great faith in her judgment and her ability to help. Now he was certain that she could find a way for him to make West Point.

At first Mrs. MacArthur did not believe the doctor, for she had always thought of Douglas as being almost perfect physically. The doctor must have done something to him in the examination. He must have pinched that nerve himself, in his punching and probing.

"But what shall I do?" moaned Douglas. "I can't give up going to West Point."

"Well, first of all we'll see another doctor, but not an army doctor this time. We'll go to a bone and nerve specialist, the best there is in Milwaukee."

The specialist agreed with the army doctor. First, Douglas must have an operation to free the nerve. Then he must take exercises to help his muscles work again.

"What caused it?" asked his mother.

The specialist shrugged his shoulders and looked at the tall, sturdy boy sitting on the table. "Possibly football," he replied. "This happens now and then in a hard game."

"How long will it take to get over the operation?" Douglas asked.

"Possibly years," the doctor said. "We'll see how the muscles respond."

"It can't take that long because I'm going to West Point next year!"

"Hm. Well, we'll see about that when the time comes. Much will depend upon you, and how hard you work at your own cure."

"Don't worry! I'll work hard!"

A year later the specialist said Douglas was cured. He could go to West Point.

"The workout you'll get there should strengthen your muscles and make you all the stronger," the specialist said.

When Mrs. MacArthur accompanied her

younger son to enter West Point, the *Milwaukee Journal* marked their going with this item:

Douglas MacArthur has received the highest mark for his appointment to West Point. His standing was 93.3 while the next highest had a score of 77.9. He scored 700 out of a possible 750 points.

Douglas realized from his record that it paid to be prepared. Now that he was entering West Point, he must be prepared for many things to come. His brother Arthur had explained to him about hazing.

"Of course you must expect to be hazed," Arthur had written. "You can make life much easier by keeping your mouth closed in the presence of upper classmen. Do willingly whatever they may ask you to do, even though it may seem silly to you. Your first six weeks will be the worst."

At West Point the freshmen were called

fourth classmen or plebes, and the sophomores were called third classmen or yearlings. Douglas was not surprised when the yearlings began to make life miserable for the plebes. The yearlings considered it their duty to teach the plebes how to take orders and to be obedient. Men who couldn't take orders had no business in West Point. They wouldn't make good officers.

The United States Military Academy at West Point had one important purpose—to train young men to be the best military officers in the world. This purpose could not be accomplished unless the students were ambitious and willing to take the training they needed.

The first lesson a young man had to learn at West Point was obedience. He had to obey promptly and without question any order that might be given. All officers, regardless of rank, had to obey their superior officers. Even generals had to obey the Commander-in-Chief, who was the President of the United States. The President had to obey the people.

The third classmen had strange ways of teaching the plebes obedience. For two full months they made the plebes their slaves.

After two weeks at West Point, the new cadets, or fourth classmen, were lined up on the parade ground under the direction of upper class officers. There, with their eyes on the flag fluttering feebly in the breeze, they agreed to follow the motto of the Academy, *Duty, Honor, Country*. The cadets promised solemnly to protect the United States of America with their lives. They were now in the army.

The next day the cadets were moved into Boot Camp, where each company had its own street of tents. Each cadet was assigned to serve a third classman or sophomore during his training at the camp. He had to make the third classman's bed, run his errands, carry his laundry, polish his brass, brush his uniform, shine his shoes, and even adjust his tent flaps so that the rain or sun could not disturb him.

In addition, he had to do any exercises his third classman or any other upper classmen might order him to do, at any time, in any place. He had to obey without speaking or objecting in any way. He was told that sudden demands for physical exercise of various kinds were "for the good of the Corps."

Sometimes a cadet was aroused from sleep in the night to carry out orders. Third classmen, who had been treated harshly by upper classmen the year before, took special pleasure in making unreasonable demands.

If a fourth classman refused to do what the upper classmen ordered, he was required to fight an upper classman, picked for the purpose by a committee of third classmen. Naturally the upper classman, made tough by at least one year of hard physical exercise, always won when a fight took place. Each plebe knew that it was much easier to obey than to fight. If he chose to fight, he had to fight until he was beaten so badly that he couldn't get up to fight longer. He had to give up.

Some upper classmen did not wish to haze their "special duty men." They were satisfied to have the men act as servants. Douglas had hoped to get an upper classman of this sort, but he drew the opposite. His superior was a young southerner, named Dockery, who was bitter because his parents had lost their plantation in the War between the States. Dockery considered Douglas arrogant and conceited.

"He's the most conceited man I ever saw," Dockery confided to a classmate. "I'll take the conceit out of him, if it takes a year."

One night Dockery wakened Cadet MacArthur and ordered him to come outside.

"Eagles," ordered Dockery. "A hundred eagles——and make them fast."

Douglas stifled a yawn and stood on his toes, his arms held out, making a cross of his body. Then he bent his knees almost to the ground, flapping his arms. Next he drew himself half way up and then bent low again, all without losing his balance. This routine completed one eagle. It was hard to keep steady for one or two eagles, but Douglas was supposed to complete a hundred eagles!

Douglas knew that he had to obey his superior officer. A hundred eagles it would be. At first it really felt good to stretch, especially outside in the cool night air. It was much cooler outside than inside the crowded tent.

"Count out loud," ordered Dockery.

"Six—seven—eight—nine——"

"Keep counting!"

"Twenty-five—twenty-six—" Douglas found

80

it harder and harder to count. It wasted breath that was becoming more and more precious.

By forty-nine he began to feel himself trembling. He thought of the year he had spent, making his back strong. Now he fully understood what the medical officer had meant about the strenuous exercises at West Point.

Still he went on counting, trembling more and more with every bend. Everything began to blur and to go round and round. Then he felt a sharp pain in his spinal cord.

"Fifty-five, sixty—fifty-five, sixty—" He could scarcely remember what number came next. "Sixty-four, sixty-five—" He tried to keep on counting, but finally had to give up. Then he heard himself moan, and he felt himself sinking, down, down, down. Wonderful! Wonderful! Now there wasn't any pain.

Douglas woke up in the camp infirmary. A few white-faced cadets stood beside his bed.

"Thank God you've come to!" moaned Dockery. "I didn't know—really, I hadn't any idea you'd have convulsions."

Douglas sat up in bed. "Convulsions!" he cried, speaking freely to the upper classmen. "What are you talking about?"

The others nodded. "We thought you'd never stop twitching," said one of them.

"We put some cotton in your mouth to keep you from biting your tongue. Doc said the convulsions were caused because you didn't get enough air to keep going. We didn't know."

"No," said Dockery. "We didn't know."

The superintendent sent for Mrs. MacArthur to tell her what had happened to Douglas. Of course, she was greatly disturbed.

"What are you doing to my boy, Colonel Mills?" she demanded.

"Is there any history of falling sickness in your family?" he asked.

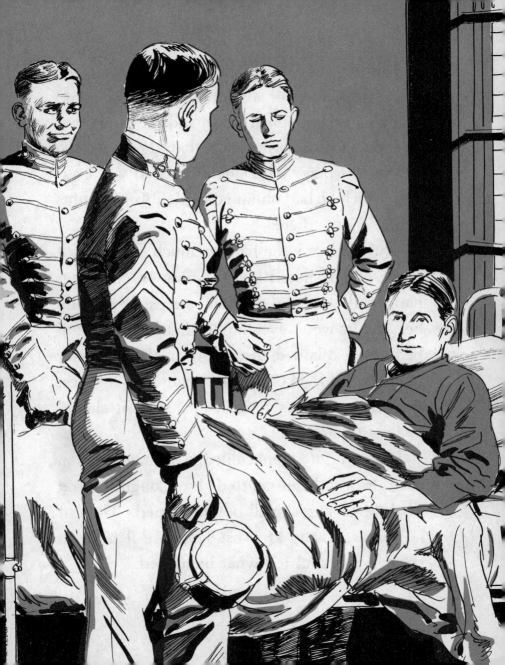

This question made her so angry that she couldn't answer for a moment. Then she told him about the pinched nerve and the operation, and the doctor's assurance that there was no reason to worry. All Douglas needed was exercise, which he had obtained in plentiful amounts before coming here.

"Evidently my son had too much exercise last night, and I should like to know exactly what happened," she said. "There's no use to ask him because he won't even admit that he was out of bed. He explained that being in the infirmary today is just a joke. If the hazing here at West Point is as bad as I think that it is, it should be investigated."

The superintendent smiled. "An investigation has already been started by Congress, and doubtless Douglas will be questioned. Then, if he wants to stay at West Point, he'll have to speak freely and tell what happened."

84

"He wants to stay," said Mrs. MacArthur. "He wants to spend his whole life in the army."

"Then tell him he'd better talk."

"That's up to him, but he won't want to get his superiors into trouble."

"No, of course not, but he'll have to answer questions, or else be dismissed. There's no way around it."

"I'll warn Dougie, so that he can think things over in advance."

The Hard Decision

Slowly Cadet MacArthur opened an envelope from the *United States Congress*. He knew what was inside and wished that he didn't have to open it. He wished that he had never received it. "You are hereby notified. . . ."

Tomorrow! The hearing was to take place the next day. He wondered what questions would be asked and what answers he should give. At supper time he got permission to visit his mother. He wanted her advice. He wanted her to tell him what he should say.

"If the committee asks me to name names, I'll refuse," he said. "Besides, why is Congress sending a committee here? Why is it snooping into our affairs here at West Point?"

"Congress is paying the bills, Doug, and has a right to ask questions."

"Well, then, I have a right to refuse to answer their questions."

"Which gives the officers a right to dismiss you from West Point. Have you thought of that and the possibility of leaving?"

He hadn't. It was a frightening thought. "Do you mean that I should name names?"

"You'll have to decide, and it will be a hard decision to make. On the other hand, if you're going to become a good officer, you'll have to learn to make hard decisions. There is no easy road to success in the army or anywhere else."

"Can the officers really dismiss me for not telling who made me do the eagles?"

"They can. They will, too, if they think you are being arrogant."

"Well, I don't care what they do to me. I don't want to tell."

"You're sure of that? You'd be willing to leave here—under a cloud perhaps?"

"I don't know. I just don't know."

"You'll have to make up your mind, son. It must be your own choice, not mine. Go back to your barracks now and get a good night's rest. Maybe by morning you will have decided. If it will help any, you can know that I have faith in you. You'll make the right choice."

"What is right? I'm not sure."

"You will be, when the time comes."

Douglas slept little that night, and the next morning couldn't eat breakfast. He felt sick, just as he had the morning before he took his West Point examination.

Even though he was nervous, he had decided what to do. He would answer questions, so long as they were about himself, but he wouldn't tell about others. If he was dismissed for refusing to answer, he would just have to go. Certainly he wouldn't want to stay on, knowing that his words had caused someone to be dismissed. Several men from last year's third class had already been dismissed for hazing.

The congressional committee met in the office of the superintendent. The members had arrived the night before and had been entertained with a party. Mrs. MacArthur had attended the party, but Douglas hadn't talked with her to find out what the men were like. He must meet them and answer their questions without knowing them. She wanted it that way.

The committee members looked very grim as they sat around the superintendent's long table.

"State your name," said the chairman.

"Douglas MacArthur, sir."

"Your age?"

"Nineteen, sir."

"Your class?"

"Fourth, sir."

"Is it true, sir, that the members of your class have been subjected to hazing by the members of the class above you?"

"Every new class is hazed, sir. Hazing is a part of our training as well as our studies."

"Have you yourself been subjected to hazing since you have been here?"

"Yes, sir."

"Tell us about one certain night when you were hazed. You know what night I mean?"

"I think so, sir."

Douglas calmly told about the night he had been wakened from sleep and ordered into the company street to do "eagles." He spread out his arms and bent his knees to show exactly what an eagle was. He felt a little proud of himself for being able to demonstrate an eagle so well. Not a muscle in his body quivered.

"Did you do the one hundred eagles?"

"No, sir."

"How many did you do?"

"I don't remember, sir."

"Why don't you remember?"

"I blacked out, sir, but I can do them now. I have proved that I can."

"We would like you to tell us, Cadet Mac-Arthur, the name of the third classman who wakened you and ordered you to do this exercise."

"I'm sorry, sir, but I cannot give you his name. I cannot report against my superior."

The committee members frowned and looked inquiringly at one another. The chairman made little beats on the table with his fingers.

"Evidently you don't realize the seriousness of what you are saying, Cadet MacArthur. You are defying the United States of America when you refuse to answer our questions."

"I'm sorry, sir. I still can't answer."

"Do you understand that you can be dismissed for this defiance?"

"I don't mean to be defiant, sir. I just can't name the cadet, sir."

"Suppose this same young man should happen to be plotting an act of treason? Would you still protect him?"

"That would be very different, sir. I hope that I shall never have to make a decision of that sort. This one has been hard enough."

"I ask you again, young man, under threat of dismissal. What was the name of the man who did the hazing?"

Douglas stood at attention, his lips pressed tightly as if determined.

"Tell us, Cadet MacArthur, why you so stubbornly refuse to answer our questions."

"My mother advised me to think this thing through, sir, and I have tried to do so. From my earliest childhood, I have been taught not to tattle. Giving the cadet's name to you in this investigation, it seems to me, would come under that head. In a sense my whole life's training is at stake here.

"I know the consequences, if I refuse to answer you, but I believe I would deserve dismissal more for telling than for not telling. It seems to me that a cadet with so little loyalty would make a poor officer. I hope you'll let me stay here, because I'll make a far better officer for having proved my loyalty now."

The faces of the committee members softened a little. They realized that his arguments made sense and that he would make a good officer. Hazing hadn't hurt him. He was still top man in his class. Why waste more time on him?

"Take him back to his quarters," growled the chairman. "We're getting nowhere. Furthermore, we can get the information from other cadets when we interview them."

Cadet MacArthur sighed with relief. He saluted the committee, with his chin pressed in and his body erect.

"Thank you, sir. Thank you very much. I—— I would certainly hate to leave here."

The committee continued its investigation and recommended a change in the cadet code, so that new cadets could be hardened, but not persecuted by their upper classmen.

When June came, Douglas stood first in his class and Ulysses S. Grant III, grandson of U. S. Grant, former General and President, second. The next year, he was first again and Grant was second. The third year they still ranked high, but slightly lower than before. Douglas was fourth, and Grant was sixth.

During his third year Cadet MacArthur began to take greater interest in social events. He was a handsome young man to behold, a good dancer, and an interesting talker.

There were many interesting social affairs at West Point during the year. There were football and baseball games and Saturday night dances, usually called hops. Then over the weekends, there were hikes about the grounds.

No young ladies attended West Point, because it was a men's school. Young ladies came to the campus, however, to accompany the cadets on social events. Some of the young ladies came from nearby homes and schools. Others were sisters and friends from the home communities.

During his years as an upper classman, Douglas met many of these young ladies. He was very popular with them, for he was sure each girl he dated was lovelier than the last one.

As in other matters, Mrs. MacArthur frequently talked with Douglas about his future married life. "It takes a special kind of girl to make a good army wife," she said. "She must be willing to take a back seat and let her husband be in the limelight. You can't find that kind of person everyday.

"The wrong kind of wife can ruin a man's career," Mrs. MacArthur continued, "but the right kind of wife can help him make a career."

While Douglas was a second classman, West Point celebrated its hundredth birthday. President Theodore Roosevelt, who was a friend of Douglas' father, came up to review the Corps and make the graduation speech. Roosevelt had been Vice President under President William McKinley. When McKinley was murdered by an assassin, Roosevelt had become President.

Douglas and Ulysses Grant III were appointed "special duty men" for the President. They brought his shaving water and made his bed. They blacked his boots and brushed his clothes. Somehow they felt happy doing the same things for the President that they had found difficult to do for third classmen when they were plebes.

The President watched the Army baseball team play a game with a team from Yale University. Douglas played shortstop and hit a home run in the game. The Army team won because the Yale men couldn't match the hardened cadets.

Douglas had never played any better. He always played best when there was a good audience, and today he was playing for his Commander-in-Chief, a friend of his father.

The President spoke to the cadets. "This institution," he said, "has completed its first hundred years. During that hundred years no other educational institution in the land has given as many names as West Point to the honor roll of the nation's great citizens.

"Your duty here at West Point has been to fit men to do well in war. But it is also a well-known fact that you have also fitted them to do unusually well in peace."

During the commencement exercises, the second year classmen watched the members of the Class of 1902 get their diplomas. The graduates were the same persons who had tormented them when they were plebes.

"It's our turn next," they said to one another. Then they went to pack their bags for a long summer furlough.

Douglas liked West Point, but he was happy because there was only one more year to go. Soon he would be on his own.

Lieutenant
MacArthur

Douglas had hoped that he and his mother could spend the summer with his father, who now was Military Governor of the Philippines. They gave up going, however, because the trip would take so long that they would have little time to spend with General MacArthur. Most of the trip would consist of a long boat ride.

Besides, General MacArthur had confided in a letter to Mrs. MacArthur that the control of the Philippines was going to be transferred. President McKinley had appointed William Howard Taft Governor General of the Philippines to take the place of General MacArthur.

100

Ever since the Spanish American War, the Philippines had been under military rule. Now the government had decided to end the military rule and to place the islands under civil authority. Taft was a civil officer. General MacArthur would have to work under the direction of Taft. MacArthur was no longer in complete charge.

Under the United States Constitution, civil authority ranks higher than military authority. The President of the United States is Commander-in-Chief of the United States Army. The United States cannot be ruled by the army or any branch of the armed services.

General MacArthur had hoped to continue as Military Governor of the Philippines. He did not want the islands to be put under a civil governor. He disagreed with some of Taft's plans for governing the islands. Finally he was transferred from the Philippines to a station in San Francisco, California.

Douglas and his mother were glad to have General MacArthur in the United States again. Now they could see him from time to time without having to make a long ocean journey. Also, they were glad to have him here while Douglas spent his last year in school. The general probably could come to commencement.

A few months after General MacArthur came home from the Philippines, President Roosevelt asked Taft to become Secretary of War in his cabinet. Then the President ordered a great celebration to welcome Taft back to the United States. He asked General MacArthur to make the arrangements for this celebration.

General MacArthur worked hard to prepare the celebration for Taft. He blamed Taft for causing his dismissal from the Philippines, but didn't let his feelings interfere with call to duty. He even rode in an open carriage with Taft during the celebration.

The next June Taft as Secretary of War came to West Point to present diplomas to the graduates. The first name to be called was that of Douglas MacArthur. Douglas was top man in the class. He had made the highest grades ever made by any student at West Point. He had received many honors as a student.

Secretary of War Taft read all the honors Cadet MacArthur had received. There was a great burst of applause when he finished reading. Douglas was the most popular man in his class, as the great applause showed. He also was popular throughout the academy.

Douglas walked to the platform in fine military form. He looked straight into the eyes of the Secretary of War. Then he saluted and politely took his diploma.

Seated on the platform with other important persons was General MacArthur, Douglas' father. After Douglas received his diploma, he paused for a moment and walked over to where his father was seated. Then he bowed deeply and handed his diploma to his father, who was greatly surprised. Finally, ignoring Taft's outstretched hand, he marched to his seat.

This surprise action delighted General Mac-Arthur, because it showed how much Douglas respected him. Douglas felt very proud of both his father and mother. He also felt indebted to them for their encouragement and guidance.

When Douglas graduated, he became a second lieutenant in the United States Army. He was listed as an engineer and given his choice of a station. He chose the Philippine Islands, largely because his father had been stationed there and he felt that he would enjoy being there.

Douglas immediately fell in love with the Philippines. Somehow he seemed to have the strange feeling that he had been there before. Also he seemed to feel that he was headed for many adventures. His father had told him interesting stories about the two ancient forts on the islands, Bataan and Corregidor. Here the noted Filipino rebel, Aguinaldo, and his followers had defied American guns for many weeks.

The people, who had known General Mac-Arthur, welcomed Douglas to the Philippines. They made him feel that this was his home.

The army engineers were building barracks and docks in the Philippines. The wood which they were using had to be cut in the jungle. A short time after the new lieutenant arrived, he was placed in charge of a detail that was clearing a section of the jungle.

One day Lieutenant MacArthur had gone ahead to mark trees to be cut. Suddenly, out of nowhere, almost as if dropped from the sky, two angry Filipinos stood on either side of him. Their guns were pointed straight at his head. Needless to say, he was greatly surprised.

Suddenly he remembered from his training in Indian warfare how he had been taught to draw a gun quickly. As he reached for his gun, one of the Filipinos fired. The shot knocked Mac-Arthur's hat from his head. Then he shot before the second man could fire. First one, and then two men lay on the ground beside him.

The first sergeant under the lieutenant's command came running at the sound of the shots. The two men on the ground, the hat with the bullet hole in it, and the still smoking gun told the story. For a minute all the sergeant could do was to look at the scene before him.

"Beggin' the lieutenant's pardon, the rest of his life is velvet," he said with a grin.

At that moment Douglas remembered the Indian arrow he had tried so hard to catch. He remembered how his mother had told him that God had spared his life for some great purpose.

It was beginning to look, he thought, as if she might be right. He was beginning to wonder what that great purpose would be.

A Trip to Asia

In 1904 THE Russo-Japanese War began. The Japanese navy attacked the Russian navy at Port Arthur in Manchuria.

Russia had been building the Trans-Siberian Railroad eastward across Asia. Wood for building the railroad was being obtained from Chinese territory along the Yalu River.

Several years before, Japan and China had fought a war over territory which both countries claimed. After the war, Russia had helped these two countries to draw up a treaty. In this treaty, Port Arthur had been taken away from Japan and given to China.

Japan feared that Russia was trying to take over China, and tried to get Russia out by peaceful means, but failed. Now it seemed to be necessary to fight.

President Roosevelt sent a party of army and navy officers to Japan to investigate the trouble. One of the officers in the party was General MacArthur. General MacArthur asked to take his son along as his aide. By now Douglas had been promoted to first lieutenant.

Young MacArthur enjoyed his trip to Japan and learned many important things while he was there. He made friends among the Japanese people and came to know how they lived.

Once while he was with his father, he had an opportunity to see the Japanese fight a battle. He watched a company of men force their way up a hill, under the direct fire of the Russians. Not a man wavered. Only the fallen men did not follow their leader. It was impossible for men to demonstrate greater courage or greater determination to reach a goal.

When the war was over, President Roosevelt asked General MacArthur to remain abroad to observe conditions throughout Asia. He was promoted by a special act of Congress to lieutenant general. Again he took his son with him as his aide.

Young MacArthur, traveling with his father, visited many countries in Asia. He listened eagerly as his father talked with the heads of government and military leaders. He found out how the countries tried to take advantage of one another and often started wars. He found out that it was difficult to keep peace.

By the time young MacArthur returned to the United States, he was greatly interested in the countries of Asia. He felt that many important things would happen there.

He was especially interested in Japan, and

read all that he could about the country. He read how Japan had been separated from the rest of the world for many years, but was now becoming a world power.

When young MacArthur went back to the United States, he joined an army engineer school at Washington, D. C. This school had been opened to train officers in the newest military discoveries. After seeing fighting in a real war, he realized that he still had much to learn. He was happy to be enrolled in the school to learn as much as he could.

While he studied at the engineer school, he served as one of the White House aides to President Roosevelt. Serving as an aide gave him an opportunity to see many important people who came to Washington.

Douglas made an exceptionally good aide to the President. He looked very neat and attractive in his uniform. He was polite and thought-

111

ful. He was mannerly, knew his way about, and made few mistakes. Also he admired the President and was eager to carry out his wishes. He was close to the President's sons.

At the White House Douglas often had an opportunity to talk with the President. He told the President what he had seen and learned in Asia, especially in Japan. Now and then visitors from Asia, whom he had met before in their home countries, came to the White House.

In 1908 the people of the United States elected William Howard Taft to succeed Roosevelt as President. General MacArthur, remembering his earlier disagreements with Taft, resigned from the army. He and Mrs. MacArthur left Washington and moved to Milwaukee, Wisconsin. Then in 1912 he died after a short illness.

Captain Douglas MacArthur now was stationed at Fort Leavenworth, Kansas. His father's death was a great shock to him, but he continued to move ahead. Within a short time he was promoted to major and given a new assignment. This assignment was exactly what he wanted. He became a junior engineer officer on the Army Board. Now he would live in Washington, D. C., and his mother could come to live with him.

World War I

WHEN WORLD WAR I started in 1914, young MacArthur was given a desk job in Washington. He was to work with newspapermen to make certain that they prepared proper reports.

"The people want to know what's going on," he told the reporters when he held his first meeting. "You should see that they know the truth, except in cases that might give aid and comfort to the enemy."

In his meetings with the reporters, young MacArthur was careful to explain the news clearly. He wanted to be sure that people would understand what was happening.

As the war continued, young MacArthur decided that he wanted to go overseas. He wanted to go to Europe, where he could take part in the fighting. He was unhappy holding a desk job, when other men were going to Europe.

The Secretary of War at this time was Newton D. Baker. One day he came to see young MacArthur in his office.

"I've a question to ask you," said the Secretary of War.

Douglas put down his pen, turned his chair, and looked up in surprise. "What question do you wish to ask me?" he said. "Am I supposed to know the answer?"

"Maybe. At least, no one else does. Do you think the reserves could hold up under fire if they were sent overseas?"

"Of course they could if they were trained properly," he answered. "Why?"

"Some people don't agree with you."

"Well, I know some of the reserves. The boys from Washington and Texas would hold up under fire, I am sure."

The secretary interrupted. "What would you think of a division made up of selected reserves from every state in the Union?"

"A wonderful idea! This kind of division would be like a great rainbow, sweeping across the whole country."

"Good!" said the Secretary of War. "We'll call it the Rainbow Division."

Secretary Baker left, but in a few minutes he came back. "Major, come with me. I want you to tell President Wilson about our plans for the Rainbow Division."

Mr. Wilson was pleased. "I like the idea of the Rainbow Division," he said.

When the new division was organized a few weeks later, Major MacArthur was appointed staff officer of the division.

The division sailed to France in December, 1917. Douglas MacArthur was now a colonel. For the first time in his life, he was in command of troops who would soon be fighting.

What would his troops need to know? What could he teach them to help them defeat the enemy and yet preserve their own lives? He realized that they were green soldiers, not used to the army. He felt a grave responsibility to take care of them at this time.

When the men landed in France, they found that no preparations had been made for them. America had just entered the war, and there hadn't been time to get things done. The division was off to a bad start.

The weather was bitterly cold and the men had very little heat in their quarters. They lacked adequate food and clothing. Even so, Colonel MacArthur was not discouraged. He started his program of training immediately.

"Valley Forge was a picnic compared with this," said a war-hardened sergeant.

The training continued. All the while the men had to live in trenches dug in the ground. Often the trenches were filled with mud, sleet, and snow. The staff officers lived in hotels and slept in real beds. Colonel MacArthur longed to get to the front where he could live with his men in the trenches.

One day he asked permission to go to the front on a tour of inspection. He had heard a rumor that the French were getting ready to attack the Germans, and he hoped to see and possibly take part in some of the fighting. At first the permission was refused, but he insisted that it was important.

"How can I train men without seeing where they'll have to fight?" he asked.

Finally the permission was granted. A French officer told Colonel MacArthur about some of the rules of trench warfare and gave him some clippers for cutting wire. MacArthur joined a small number of raiders and started for the front. Soon they came to barbed wire stretched across the land to protect the German troops, who were hidden in trenches. They cut the barbed wire, kept on going, and soon found themselves almost on top of the trenches.

The raiders jumped into the trenches and fought hand-to-hand until the Germans either ran away or were killed. When the raid was over, the French had captured the trenches.

There was rejoicing at headquarters. The Frenchmen kissed Colonel MacArthur first on one cheek, then on the other, even though his cheeks were covered with mud. The French commander pinned the Croix de Guerre, a French medal for bravery, on his jacket. The soldiers warmed their shivering bodies around a fire. "Vive L'Americain!" they shouted.

The general at the main American army headquarters heard of Colonel MacArthur's bravery
and recommended that he be awarded the Dis-
tinguished Service Cross. Now in his first real
encounter, he had won two decorations!

One of the staff officers scolded him for taking the risk. "Why did you do it?" he asked.
"Why did you risk your life?"

"It's all in the game," Colonel MacArthur answered. Somehow he felt relieved because he
had taken the same risk that he would ask his
men to take later.

After a month the Rainbow Division was at
the front, and Douglas MacArthur had become
General MacArthur. Even though he had been
promoted and won decorations, he still wanted
to stay at the front with his men.

Two days after the Rainbow Division had
been sent to the front, some troops were ordered
to capture a section of woods. The Germans

were defending this area with batteries of guns. General MacArthur advised the company officers and led the attack in person. He took off his overcoat and tossed it into a nearby bush, so that he would have greater freedom. He moved from one spot to another.

The soldiers liked to have their general take risks with them. They recognized him by his long muffler and his cap. His cap had a funny, droopy look. He had taken out the stiffening that held the cap in shape.

"It feels better this way," he explained. He had no use for the steel helmets that were supposed to provide protection.

General MacArthur led his men up a hill, under heavy enemy fire. There was something about his cap that gave the men courage. They knew he would lead them with all possible regard for their safety.

When he started up the hill, he wasn't sure

that the men would follow him. The enemy fire was terrible. For a moment he slowed down to see whether the men were coming. Then in a few seconds he saw them stumbling toward him. On and on he went with his men until the hill was taken and the battle was won.

At three o'clock in the morning, a tired young general came into headquarters, pushing five German officers before him. His uniform, which had been neat and clean when he started, was now dirty and torn. Pieces of his uniform were still sticking to the barbed wire fences, which he and his prisoners had climbed through on the way to headquarters. He no longer seemed to be the trim general he had been before.

When he had given his account, the general at the headquarters said, "This should get you another decoration, Doug."

But General MacArthur was fast asleep. He did not hear what the general had said.

The next morning he went back to look for his overcoat. He found the coat, put it on, and started back to camp. By the time he arrived, he knew he had made a mistake. The overcoat had been gassed.

For four months General MacArthur was in the hospital, but he was out again in time to help drive back a German attack at Reims. By the end of the war, he had collected more medals than any other man in the army. He had won a name for himself among his own troops as "the bravest man in the world."

As a reward for his bravery, he was recommended for the Medal of Honor.

Superintendent
at West Point

GENERAL MACARTHUR came home from France
wearing the same droopy cap his men had
learned to know and to follow. Other men had
worn steel helmets for protection, but not General MacArthur.

During the war he had won thirteen military
decorations, including the Croix de Guerre, but
he still continued to wear the old cap. His
mother suggested that he get a new one.

"I like this cap," he always answered. "Why
should I get a new one?"

Finally a friend promised Mrs. MacArthur he
would urge her son to buy a new cap.

"Doug," the friend said, "you've been appointed Superintendent at West Point. Now you'll have to get a new cap. You can't expect the cadets to keep their uniforms spic and span, if they see you in that old cap."

So General MacArthur bought a new cap. He realized that he must set a good example for the cadets, if he expected them to be neat.

In a report General Pershing had said, "Douglas MacArthur is the finest military leader we have ever known." This report probably helped MacArthur get the appointment, which was a great honor, at West Point.

The war in Europe had caused much confusion at West Point. The army had needed officers so badly that many cadets with only three years of training had been given commissions. Now that the war was over, these young men were supposed to come back to finish school.

These young veterans felt much older in years

and experience than young men just coming out of high schools. They objected strongly to following the same rules as the young men who had never taken part in a war. They felt that returning to school after having commanded men on a battlefield was like being sent back to the lower grades in school.

First, General MacArthur strengthened the honor system that had long been established at West Point. According to this honor system, a cadet is trusted. His written or spoken word is regarded as the truth. He does not lie, cheat, or steal. If he shows that he cannot be trusted in some manner, he must write a written report of his wrongdoing.

For wrongdoing, a cadet must risk being sent home. It is his duty to report wrongdoing on the part of others as well as himself.

General MacArthur made changes in the West Point course of study. The war had shown that future officers needed to be taught new and different things. They needed to learn more about other countries and more about modern weapons and machines. Above all, they should know more about airplanes, which seemed to have great possibilities in warfare.

General MacArthur made physical education a vital part of school work. He composed the following motto, which appears above the entrance to the gymnasium at West Point.

"Upon the playing fields of friendly strife
Are sown the seed that,
Upon other fields, in other days
Will bear the fruits of victory."

His work was strenuous, but General Mac-Arthur liked being at West Point again. It was a great change, however, from the kind of life he had led in Europe during the war.

The money for supporting the United States Military Academy at West Point is appropriated

128

by Congress. After the war Congress was tired of appropriating large sums for military purposes. The members wanted to forget about war, hoping that none would ever come again. General MacArthur had difficulty getting Congress to appropriate enough money for West Point.

In seeking funds, General MacArthur had to make many trips to Washington. Often while he was there, he went to see General Pershing, his former commanding officer in Europe. He and Pershing had been friends for a great many years. He also came to know many other important persons in Washington.

The Bonus
Expedition

In 1930 Douglas MacArthur was appointed
Chief of Staff of the United States Army. He
was the youngest man in United States history
to be named Chief of Staff, the highest military
position he could have.

At this time the country was suffering from a
great business depression. Many banks, factories, and stores had closed and gone out of
business. People everywhere were out of work.

Farmers were forced to sell their grain and
livestock at very low prices. Money was very
difficult to get.

General MacArthur, the new Chief of Staff,

faced the problem of getting enough money for the army. He felt that the country should not allow the army to become weak even though the nation was having a business depression.

The members of Congress were busy studying ways to get banks, factories, and stores to open again so that people could find work and earn money. They weren't much interested in building a strong army.

General MacArthur outlined many things that he thought Congress should do for the army. He felt that every branch of the armed services should have its own war machines. The men needed to become acquainted with these machines and learn how to use them.

The cavalry needed to be motorized rather than continue to use horses. The army should have separate planes from the navy.

All these changes would cost money. General MacArthur explained that the country might lose the next war unless the changes were made. It was a mistake, he argued, to appropriate money for business and to neglect the army. The country would be weakened without a good army.

The size of the army had been greatly reduced after the war. Many former soldiers were now out of work. They and their families were hungry and destitute. Some felt that Congress should appropriate money to help them because of their services in the army. They insisted that Congress pay them a bonus.

Congress, handicapped because of the bad business conditions, failed to take action on the bonus. Many members felt that the veterans should be rewarded for their past services in the army. Others felt that they owed it to their country to fight during the war.

Finally unemployed veterans from many parts of the country began to come to Washington to press their claims for a bonus. They were shabbily dressed, some wearing the same old uniforms that they had worn during the war. They had little or no money in their pockets.

At one time there were twenty thousand unemployed ex-soldiers in Washington. They had come from all over America, from Illinois, from Oklahoma, from Maryland, from Colorado, from California, from every state in the Union. All were unhappy and felt that they were being mistreated by the government.

The former soldiers called themselves the Bonus Expeditionary Force. They had lost their jobs when the business failures took place, and felt that by coming they might get Congress to pass the bonus. Some of them knew congressmen from their own parts of the country.

The veterans set up a camp in a big Washington park. They wanted to stay together so they could visit and make plans. They wanted to tell their troubles to one another.

Some of the veterans moved into empty houses around the edge of the park. Most of these houses belonged to the government and were supposed to be torn down. Nobody had lived in them for years and they were badly run down. A few veterans made shelters out of wooden boxes and orange crates.

After a time the government ordered the bonus marchers to vacate the old houses on government property. The marchers ignored the orders and continued to stay. They argued that Washington was their capital and they had a right to be there. Nobody wanted them there, but nobody wanted to force them to leave.

Gradually the men began to commit crimes and became harder to control. They threw rocks, killing and injuring a number of people. They ignored the laws and frequently clashed with the police. At last the police were forced to throw up their hands.

Finally the government took action. General MacArthur, as Chief of Staff, was ordered to drive the bonus army out of the city. This was a very difficult assignment, but he had no choice but to proceed.

Being a soldier, he had great sympathy for the veterans. From the time the first of them came, he had arranged for them to be fed. He had ordered movable kitchens from the army to provide food for them. He had wanted them to be as comfortable as possible.

Now he had orders to drive the men from the city. He wondered how to do this without causing bloodshed. Finally he ordered five small tanks to be placed a short distance from the White House. These tanks would help to show the bonus marchers that the government was serious about ordering them to return home.

General MacArthur chose a marching unit of six hundred men to enforce the demand. He

himself marched with the men to order the bonus seekers to leave. The men carried tear gas bombs to take the place of guns. They wanted to avoid bloodshed, if at all possible.

Some of the bonus marchers fought back with sticks and clubs. One of them threw a rock that almost hit General MacArthur. By evening the entire camping area was cleared, and the veterans were on their way home. Not a one had been injured or harmed.

MacArthur ordered food for both the veterans and his own troops. He treated the veterans with the utmost respect. They asked for a half hour to get ready to leave, and he gave them an hour. He offered them gasoline and oil for their battered old cars.

The bonus marchers were very bitter about being forced to leave Washington. They hated to leave without persuading Congress to pass the bonus bill. About the time they left, Congress voted not to provide a bonus. It objected to veterans making demands for money and refused to be stampeded. Furthermore, it wanted to use its money to help business conditions.

Newspapermen took many photographs while the bonus marchers were in Washington. They took pictures of General MacArthur and his men ordering the marchers to leave. Some of the pictures showed MacArthur and his men dressed in bright new uniforms whereas the marchers were dressed in rags. These photographs stirred up much sympathy for the marchers.

The government's action caused many people to feel that the bonus marchers were treated unfairly. They objected to having former fighting men driven out of the national capital. Finally Congress passed a kind of unemployment insurance which was of great help to veterans.

That fall Franklin D. Roosevelt was elected President. He liked Douglas MacArthur and asked him to stay on as Chief of Staff. The two men had known each other for years.

About this time Manuel Quezon was elected President of the Philippines. He had known MacArthur when MacArthur had been stationed in the Philippines before. Now he wanted Mac-Arthur to come back to help reorganize the Philippine army.

MacArthur was very happy about this new assignment. He was fifty-five years old, yet he looked to be only forty. He returned to the Philippines with all the enthusiasm he had felt when he first entered West Point as a cadet.

Preparing
for War

FOR MANY YEARS the United States helped the people of the Philippines to improve their country by building factories, roads, railroads, hospitals, and schools. It wanted the Philippines to become strong enough to become an independent country.

In 1935 Congress passed a law allowing the people of the Philippines to elect their first president. The people chose Manuel Luis Quezon, one of their most capable citizens, for this important position. He was friendly to the United States and wanted to work with our country in every way possible.

President Quezon wanted the Philippines to have a strong army with modern equipment. He wanted the islands to be able to defend themselves, if they were attacked.

General MacArthur was happy when Quezon requested that he be allowed to come to the Philippines to help strengthen the Philippine army. He and Quezon knew each other and got along well together. They planned carefully the kind of army the Philippines should have and the kind of equipment the soldiers would need to carry on modern warfare.

One great problem which Quezon faced was getting money for the army. He pleaded hard for money from his government, but the people weren't much interested in training an army and purchasing ships and guns. They didn't think their country would be attacked or that they would ever need to fight a war.

MacArthur tried to get funds from Congress,

but he, too, had difficulty. The business depression still existed and Congress felt that all the money possible should be spent to help business. There were rumors that Japan was getting ready to start a major war, but the people weren't greatly disturbed about that, either.

In 1937 General MacArthur and President Quezon took a long journey together. They visited Japan, United States, Mexico, and several other parts of the world.

Both men were frightened by what they found going on in Japan. MacArthur remembered how he had observed the Japanese soldiers during the Russo-Japanese War. He recalled how Japan, even though small and weak, had won this war against Russia, big and strong.

Now Japan was securing large quantities of iron ore from Manchuria, a territory which the Japanese controlled in eastern Asia. The Japanese government was collecting large quantities of coal, oil, food, and other supplies from many parts of the world.

The two men saw tanks, ships, and airplanes being built. They saw huge stockpiles of food and ammunition. They saw regiments of soldiers drilling. Japan already was fighting a border war with China, but evidently was preparing to fight a much greater war. If Japanese forces should attack the Philippines, the islands could not be defended.

President Quezon hoped that the Japanese would not attack the Philippines. Japan wanted oil, coal, and other minerals, but the Philippines had none of these materials.

"The Philippines have no minerals, but they have many other things," said General MacArthur. "They grow large quantities of rice and other foods. They are well located to make a good supply base for fighting a war. Manila Bay is one of the finest harbors in the world."

MacArthur discovered that the Japanese people were no longer friendly toward him as they had been years before when he was there. Now the people were cold and seemed to be happy when he was ready to leave.

From Japan, MacArthur came to the United States to give a report of what he had seen on his visits. He reported the huge war preparations that he had observed in Japan, but the people here were very little alarmed about the possibility of a war with Japan. They felt that Japan was a long way off, too far away to attack us. They were more interested in conditions at home.

While MacArthur was in the United States, he and Jean Faircloth, a young lady from Tennessee, were quietly married. They had made their plans several months before, while Miss Faircloth was visiting in the Philippines. The news of their wedding made headlines, for it was a surprise, even to their friends.

When General MacArthur finished his conferences in Washington, he returned to Manila. With him he took his new wife, who in the years ahead would share many hardships and triumphs by his side.

General MacArthur and his wife lived in an apartment on the top story of a hotel, overlooking beautiful Manila Bay. From their windows they could see ships entering and leaving the harbor. They could also see ships anchored at a naval base, about nine miles away.

One of the most beautiful sights from the window was Bataan Peninsula, which could be seen only when the weather was clear. One side of this peninsula formed part of the coast of Manila Bay. From a distance, it always looked green and inviting, but actually it was a dense jungle. Trees and bushes and vines were matted so closely together that a person could enter only by hacking his way through.

The ground under the vegetation was rough and treacherous. There were steep rocky hills with deep crevices to be crossed. Often these crevices in the rocks were completely hidden by the dense vegetation.

In some places there were swamps filled with black water. These swamps were infested with snakes, many of them poisonous, that slithered here and there and hissed at every disturbance. The air above was filled with swarms of mosquitoes and other insects. The mosquitoes by their bites caused people to get the dreaded disease known as malaria. There were few trails through the jungle and almost no roads. In fact, the only good road on the whole peninsula was one along the coast.

On the other side of Bataan was the China Sea. This sea was rough, even when the days were calm, and it was infested with sharks. During stormy weather, it was exceedingly dangerous.

Near the tip of Bataan was an island named Corregidor, which rose high above the water. This island, like Bataan, was rough and rocky, and covered with vegetation. Trees and other plants somehow found footholds among the rocks and managed to live. Bright-colored birds flew about and built nests in the trees. Monkeys climbed here and there among the branches and hung on the vines. Everything had the ripe smell of the jungle.

The island was five miles long and wide enough for thousands of fighting men to be stationed here. Parts of it had been cleared, and it always had an abundance of pure water. Years before, the Spanish had built a fort to prevent enemy ships from entering the bay.

The fort contained a number of underground tunnels dug through solid rock. Some of the tunnels were mere passageways, and others were large rooms. They were located on different levels and connected by stairways, yet none could be seen from the surface.

When the United States took over the Philippine Islands after the Spanish-American War, it remodeled the fort. It converted some of the rooms into quarters for dining, sleeping, and hospital purposes in case of a long siege.

In 1937 General MacArthur retired from the United States Army. In retiring, he wrote President Roosevelt, "I will, of course, be just as available for war service . . . . as I would be on the active list."

Even though he retired from the United States Army, he stayed in the Philippines to help President Quezon build up the island's defenses. He still felt that sooner or later the islands would have trouble with Japan.

In 1938 a son, Arthur, was born to the MacArthurs in Manila. They chose their friends, President and Mrs. Quezon, to be the baby's godparents and found a Chinese woman to be his nurse.

In 1939, World War II started in Europe with Germany and other countries fighting France, England, and Belgium. At the same time, Japan was openly preparing for a war to get control of more territory in the Far East.

In 1941 President Roosevelt called General MacArthur back into service. He placed him in command of the United States Army in the Far East. Then our country began to build up defenses in the Philippines.

There are more than seven thousand islands in the Philippines. MacArthur could not defend all these islands, with a limited number of soldiers. He felt that it would be better to use his forces to defend Bataan and Corregidor. These two places were important because they controlled the entrance to Manila Bay.

Ships had to pass on one side or the other of

Corregidor to enter the bay. The country that held Corregidor could attack enemy ships which tried to reach Manila.

Bataan was large enough to form a good military base. An army stationed there could hold out for a long period of time. The tip of the peninsula was only a few miles from the rocky island fort, and wounded soldiers could be brought to the hospital on Corregidor.

MacArthur ordered herds of cattle to be turned loose on the peninsula. He had caches of food and ammunition hidden there. The cattle and other supplies would be available, if he and his men needed them.

The general also established the best possible means of communication by radio, telegraph, and cable with the rest of the world. Throughout the siege that followed, these means of communication were never destroyed.

War in the Far East

On December 7, 1941, the Japanese attacked Pearl Harbor, an American naval base in Hawaii. The attack came as a surprise and great damage was done. Many American fighting men were killed and wounded, and many American ships and airplanes were destroyed. The Americans had no chance to defend themselves.

A few hours later Japanese airplanes attacked the main Philippine airfields and damaged or destroyed many American airplanes. Some American airplanes tried to fight off the Japanese airplanes, but had little chance because the enemy airplanes were so numerous.

For two weeks Mrs. MacArthur, her small son, and the other people in Manila watched the Japanese airplanes bomb and sink ships in the bay. The noise was like the sound of a thousand thunderbolts. The whole city shuddered fearfully as the bombs exploded.

The chief naval base, nine miles away, was destroyed. Old men, women, and children waited helplessly, wondering how long it would be before airplanes would bomb Manila.

Soon Japanese troops landed on the north and the west coasts of Luzon, the island on which Manila is located. MacArthur's forces attacked them and inflicted heavy losses.

A few days later, hundreds of enemy ships, carrying a huge army of Japanese fighting men, entered a gulf along the west coast of Luzon, not far from Manila. Two days later, ships carrying enemy forces, anchored along the east coast, opposite Manila bay. The Japanese general intended to divide MacArthur's forces on Luzon and destroy them.

MacArthur did not have enough troops, equipment, and supplies to fight two armies at once, one attacking from the west and another from the east. Therefore he decided to use his forces to defend Bataan and Corregidor, which would be hard to take. He already knew much about the hills, jungles, and swamps here, and could put up a strong defense.

He ordered buses, trucks, and all the other vehicles he could get, to be loaded with food, ammunition, medicines, and other things his soldiers would need. These vehicles traveled night and day from Manila, carrying supplies to Bataan. The herds of cattle, which now were scattered about the peninsula, would help to provide food. The ammunition, hidden in the rocks, would strengthen the defense.

In order to hold back the Japanese on Luzon

as long as possible, he ordered the American armies to fight outside the city of Manila. At the same time, these armies were to retreat slowly toward Bataan, so that all the forces could be combined. As the armies retreated, they were ordered to build roadblocks and destroy roads and bridges. This action would delay the enemy forces in reaching Bataan.

General MacArthur moved his headquarters to Corregidor and declared Manila an open city. He hoped the Japanese would not bomb Manila, since nothing was being done to protect it. President Quezon and his staff also moved to Corregidor to run the government.

On Christmas Eve, under the cover of darkness, Mrs. MacArthur and Arthur, who was almost four, were taken across Manila Bay to Corregidor. They had to leave the Christmas tree, which had been decorated for Arthur, in the apartment. Within four days, the Japanese

made an attack on the fort. When the warning
siren sounded, Mrs. MacArthur, her son, and the
other women were rushed to shelter in the tunnels. The house where they had been living on

the fort was destroyed. General MacArthur, himself, stood outside the tunnels and watched.

Altogether by now there were about 30,000 American and Philippino troops on Bataan and Corregidor. The men were willing to fight, but they lacked enough food, ammunition, and equipment to fight their very best. They had so few airplanes that they could provide little resistance to the Japanese bombings.

The United States tried to get help to MacArthur and his brave men, but this was almost impossible. There was little chance to bring in food, equipment, and ammunition because of the Japanese bombings. All the while the brave men fought on, against many times the number of well-fed, well-equipped Japanese troops.

Slowly the war which had started in Europe spread to other parts of the world. The Japanese were getting control of the whole Pacific. They were not only invading the Philippines but islands all over the ocean. They were bombing these islands, landing troops, conquering people, and helping themselves to food and other supplies. For a time it looked as if nothing could be done to stop them.

In Europe the German troops were still marching ahead, conquering and taking over cities and villages. German submarines were sinking so many ships that the Allies had trouble getting enough supplies to their troops.

MacArthur constantly sent messages, telling of the plight of his men. He was proud of these tired soldiers, many of them only boys, who fought like wolves at bay. He felt that they could win, if they could only get help.

After a few months the men became ragged and hungry, and many suffered from injuries and malaria. Each day the men became fewer in number from fighting and sickness, yet they fought on bravely and refused to surrender.

By now the United States had many fighting men abroad, both in Europe and in the Pacific. It faced a great problem of sending food, ammunition, and equipment to men in such distant places. Gradually the Japanese threw a great blockade around the Philippines. All the while the brave fighting men on Corregidor and Bataan were hoping that help would come.

In February, President Quezon became ill and had to leave Corregidor. He and his staff finally managed to reach the United States, where they looked after the Philippine government affairs from a distance.

Jean MacArthur had been urged to accompany President Quezon and his staff, but she refused to leave MacArthur's side. "We three are one," she said. "We drink of the same cup."

She often visited the hospital tunnels, which were overflowing with sick and wounded, to help and encourage the soldiers.

The Japanese bombings gradually became more intense. For eleven long weeks General MacArthur and his loyal troops put up a defense noted around the world.

Corregidor and Bataan were completely cut off, but their cable, telegraph, and radio communications systems remained in working order. Through these communications, General MacArthur told the world how his men were fighting from foxholes and from behind rocks, although outnumbered ten to one. He told how, sick with malaria and starving from lack of food, they continued to fight. Finally he announced that they were holding only the tip of Bataan.

Finally President Roosevelt ordered General MacArthur to go to Australia and take command of the whole Southwest Pacific area. The general hated to leave his heroic men on Corregidor and Bataan, but had no choice. He had to obey orders from his Commander-in-Chief.

The fighting of the brave men on Corregidor and Bataan had been of great help to the Allies. It had kept the Japanese from using troops, ships, and airplanes in other places. It had given the Allies time to strengthen their defenses, especially in Australia, where MacArthur was now being sent.

MacArthur planned to take his family and seventeen men with him to Australia. He decided to try to escape in four PT boats, instead of a submarine beneath the surface.

Someone suggested a brave navy lieutenant to pilot the boats. This lieutenant, who was in command of a PT boat, had recently destroyed a 5,000 ton Japanese supply ship and escaped unharmed. He was asked whether he thought that he could pilot the general's party through the treacherous Japanese-controlled waters. "Yes, on the nose, sir," he replied.

The plan called for the lieutenant to pilot the

party about six hundred miles to a hidden cove. There airplanes would be waiting to take the party the rest of the way.

"Can do, sir," he agreed, and went off to prepare for the trip.

MacArthur left the troops on Corregidor and Bataan in charge of his good friend, General Jonathan Wainwright. "Jim," he said, "hold on till I come back for you."

The general's staff boarded the PT boats, and he came with his wife and son to board one of the boats. It was night and completely dark as the four PT boats made their way through the bay, which was planted with mines.

"What's his chance, Sarge, of getting through?" someone asked.

"Dunno," was the reply. "Maybe one in five. I hope he's lucky, though."

I Shall Return

As soon as the skippers cleared the bay, they turned on full power, and the boats roared out into the China Sea. The engines on the boats sounded like airplane engines, and the Japanese failed to notice any difference.

The China Sea is rough, and the boats pitched and tossed. The winds rose, and the high waves splashed over the decks. All the passengers became soaked, and most of them became seasick. Several times they saw white flashing lights— the Japanese warning that someone was trying to escape through the blockade—but the enemy did not find them.

During the dark night on the rough sea, the four PT boats became separated. When dawn came, a dense fog hung over the sea. It was difficult to see very far.

Finally the skipper of one PT boat thought that he saw a Japanese destroyer coming in his direction. He ordered drums of gasoline to be thrown overboard and told his men to get ready to fire their torpedoes. Then fortunately he discovered that the approaching boat was not a destroyer but the PT boat in which MacArthur and his family were riding.

After the PT boat dropped most of its gasoline, it couldn't keep up with the other boats. It lacked enough fuel to keep all its engines running. Finally the skippers decided to load the passengers from this boat onto two other boats, but not the one on which the MacArthur family was riding. Then the two boats, now heavily loaded, started on.

The first PT boat arrived two hours late at the place where the skippers had agreed to hide during the day, and the second one arrived still later. The third one, which carried General Mac-Arthur and his family, had to hide in a nearby cove for a while during the day. Japanese scouting planes forced it to hide. That evening the three PT boats continued their journey.

Suddenly a Japanese cruiser appeared behind them. The skippers went ahead at full speed, hoping that the enemy would not see them or would mistake them for fishing boats. The sea became rougher and rougher, but this may have been fortunate. Enemy patrol boats, which abounded in this area, were less likely to spot the PT boats in stormy weather.

On the morning of the third day, the three boats reached the end of their six-hundred-mile voyage. Sometime later the boat that had lost some of its gasoline turned up. Its crew had

managed to bring it all the way through. An American submarine, which had been sent to these waters to check on the safety of the travelers, also showed up.

Airplanes were supposed to be waiting to take the travelers on to Australia, but no airplanes were here. Finally after three days two airplanes arrived. All the travelers crowded into these two airplanes and managed to reach Australia.

Soon after General MacArthur and his fellow travelers arrived in Australia, he made a short statement to the newspapermen. He explained that the President had ordered him to break through the Japanese lines and come from Corregidor to Australia. He had come to help protect the people of Australia from the Japanese.

He ended his statement with stirring words showing that he expected to return to Corregidor. "I came through, and I shall return," he said with great determination.

I shall return. These simple words gave hope to the starving, malaria-ridden troops who had been pushed to the very tip of Bataan. In April they were pushed off the peninsula to Corregidor, and in May, General Wainwright was forced to surrender Corregidor and his troops to the Japanese. In the prison camps they still remembered the message.

Gradually the words *I shall return* became the battle cry of the Philippino underground. They were written in huge letters on the sands of the beaches. They were scribbled on walls and sidewalks. They appeared on the windows of bombed stores and other buildings.

Thousands of copies of this message, with American and Philippino flags printed beside it, were dropped from planes or sent ashore by submarines or PT boats. Rumors spread that MacArthur was on his way, and the message struck terror among the Japanese troops.

168

General MacArthur could not return to the Philippines as soon as he had planned or hoped. In order to return, he would have to fight his way island by island for four thousand miles. The Japanese had taken over all the important islands in the Pacific.

The Allies were gradually recovering from the blows they had received early in the war. They were destroying enemy airplanes and ships and building airplanes and ships of their own. They were training more and more men for their armies and navies. They were shipping more supplies to their fighting men.

MacArthur was grateful when he began to get more fighting men, equipment, and supplies. He was especially thankful to get experienced officers to help him train and lead his men in this distant part of the world. Soon he moved his headquarters to New Guinea, which was a thousand miles nearer his goal.

On his way back, MacArthur bypassed some of the islands which the Japanese had taken. He left the enemy armies isolated, cut off from supplies and lines of communication.

Both land battles and sea battles were fought: Midway, Buna, Bismarck Sea, Guadalcanal, New Georgia, The Solomons, and many others. After a year of fierce fighting, MacArthur still was two thousand miles from Manila.

MacArthur advanced slowly until he reached islands only three hundred miles from the Philippines. Now he was within striking distance and planned to invade Leyte, one of the Philippine Islands.

On a dark night in October, 1944, General MacArthur stood on the deck of his flagship, the cruiser "Nashville," headed toward the coast of Leyte. The "Nashville" was one of a fleet of 700 American warships assembled to win back the Philippine Islands from the Japanese. These 700 ships carried about 174,000 veteran fighting men. Japan had about the same number of fighting men on the islands.

It was midnight. Thousands of American soldiers tossed in their bunks or paced the decks and peered into the darkness. Many of them wrote letters to their families at home. In the morning they would be battling the Japanese for control of the island.

As the blackness of night changed to an ugly gray, the Battle of Leyte began. Airplanes roared overhead. Ships moved toward the island with their powerful guns firing. Japanese machine guns answered.

When the sun came up, black smoke rose from the green hills of the jungle. Men waited their turn to take off on landing barges partially loaded with ammunition and supplies. There was a steady rattle of gun fire on the island as fierce fighting took place.

General MacArthur went ashore with men from the third landing barge. Several prominent Philippinos accompanied him on this landing barge. He wished that his old friend, President Quezon could have been among them, but the President had died shortly before. When the ramp was dropped about fifty yards from shore, MacArthur, with long swift strides, led the group the rest of the way to the beach.

After the battle was over, General MacArthur addressed the Filipino people on the island. They were happy to see him and gave him a tremendous welcome. They looked upon him as a friend who had come back to free them.

"People of the Philippines," said the general in addressing the crowd, "I have returned. By the grace of Almighty God, our forces stand again on Philippine soil——

"The hour of your redemption is here. . . . For your homes, and hearths, strike! For future gen-

erations of your sons and daughters, strike! In the name of your sacred dead, strike."

With this landing, the battle for the Philippines had only begun. The Japanese assembled a powerful fleet, as well as more land troops to drive the Americans out. In one great naval battle they lost three battleships and fourteen other ships. The Americans lost only about half this number of vessels.

Steady rains fell during the battles that followed. Soon the Americans landed troops on the west coast of Leyte. These troops advanced inland to join the other American forces, but the Japanese forces fought fiercely.

Luzon, the island where Manila and Bataan were located, and Corregidor were still held by the Japanese. MacArthur wanted, above all, to free the troops he had been forced to leave, and other Americans—men, women, and children—now held prisoners by the Japanese.

Finally General MacArthur directed surprise raids on Japanese prison camps to free some of the prisoners. He found his former soldiers, wasted from starvation, disease, and ill-treatment. Only a few of them were left. The others had died from the severe treatment they had received as prisoners.

The men were happy to be released from the prison camps, but some of them had bitter feelings toward MacArthur. They accused him of deserting them by going to Australia and leaving them behind. Now, as he greeted them with tears running down his cheeks, they knew that they had been wrong in their feelings.

General MacArthur walked along the corridors between their beds and spoke to them cheerfully. "You'll soon be well," he said, or "Eat all you can," or "We'll soon have the American flag flying again over Manila and Corregidor."

Although the men were frail and sick, many

of them saluted as he went by. They realized that he had fought every mile of the way back from Australia to rescue them. "You're here," they whispered, or "God bless you," or "You kept your promise."

"I'm a little late, but I'm here," he always managed to reply.

When the war started, the Filipinos scarcely realized that they could suffer so much within a short period of time. They failed to realize that modern warfare could be so destructive—— destroy so much property and take so many lives in their midst.

MacArthur had hoped to save Manila by declaring it an open city, but now it was almost completely in ruins. When the people saw MacArthur, however, they forgot the destruction about them and shouted and cried with joy. He led a triumphal procession through the city over shellholes and piles of rubble. Only the broken, charred trunks of the beautiful trees that had lined the boulevard were left.

His own apartment, including his fine library, his mother's china, priceless vases given to his father by the Emperor of Japan, and other possessions gathered over a lifetime had been destroyed. Only the family silver, which had been hidden by Filipino friends, was left.

After American troops captured Corregidor and Bataan, MacArthur held a meeting on Corregidor of all the men he had taken with him to Australia. The men stood at attention and watched the Stars and Stripes raised again on the old fort. By some strange miracle, the old flag pole had escaped damage during the war. It was almost the only thing standing.

The Japanese fought hard to keep every island, but soon all the Philippines were free. The Japanese were being defeated, but the war in the Pacific was far from over.

In the spring of 1945, President Franklin D. Roosevelt died, and Harry S. Truman became President. Within a few weeks Germany and other enemy countries in Europe surrendered. Japan still continued to fight in the Pacific.

In July, 1945, President Truman and the heads of several other countries called upon Japan to surrender. They hoped to avoid the senseless loss of life that would follow, if they had to invade Japan. Japan refused to surrender, even though gradually being defeated.

By this time the United States possessed a powerful secret weapon called the atomic bomb, which it had developed during the war. President Truman hated to use this bomb unless necessary to save the lives of American soldiers.

Early in August he issued an order for an atomic bomb to be dropped on Hiroshima, an important city in Japan. This was the first time an atomic bomb had ever been used in a war.

A few days later President Truman gave orders for a second atomic bomb to be dropped on Nagasaki, another Japanese city. Now the Japanese people realized that they would be foolish to continue the war.

On August 14, Japan surrendered. The next day the Emperor of Japan in a radio broadcast told the Japanese people that Japan had surrendered and lost the war. Dropping the bombs had brought the war to an end and saved the lives of thousands of soldiers.

General MacArthur became Supreme Commander for the Allied Powers in Japan. He flew to Japan in his plane, "Bataan," and landed on an airstrip near Tokyo. Unarmed and without guards, he stepped out to look at the conquered country. Then he made arrangements for surrender ceremonies to be held later.

One of the first persons to be released was General Jonathan Wainwright, who had been

forced to surrender at Corregidor. This heroic general was gaunt and ill, and his old uniform was two sizes too large.

Early in September, representatives of the allied countries and of the Japanese Empire gathered for the surrender ceremonies on the battleship "Missouri," anchored in Tokyo Bay. General MacArthur's hand trembled slightly as he signed the surrender papers. General Wainwright, walking feebly with a cane, attended the meeting.

The Japanese general, wearing medals and a long sword, was the last person to sign. Just as he finished, a thousand superforts and a thousand navy fighters appeared out of nowhere. These planes, which flew over the "Missouri," represented the might of the United States and the other allied countries.

The Good Leader

GENERAL MACARTHUR faced a very difficult task in helping Japan return to peaceful living. He represented an enemy country that had destroyed the Japanese army, navy, and air force, and had handed the country its first great defeat. He represented a country that had bombed Japan with a new and terrifying weapon—the atomic bomb. The Japanese people were proud of their country and their armed forces and could not readily accept defeat.

Usually when a country is defeated, it has to pay the conquering country large sums of money or products and goods of various kinds. This kind of punishment makes it continue to hate the conquering country. The people of the defeated country are very unhappy and want to fight the conquering country again as soon as possible.

MacArthur did not try to punish Japan. He wanted to help this island country become a strong peaceful nation, as soon as possible. He wanted it to be stronger than ever before and its people to be happier than ever before. He wanted the country to be a friend, not an enemy, of the United States.

The Japanese people already knew much about the United States and our way of living. For many years they had sent students to American colleges and universities. These students had returned to Japan and helped the country adopt modern ways of carrying on business and modern ways of living. They had helped the country build up trade outside Japan.

Japan was small in size, but it had a population of about 80,000,000 people. The country was overcrowded and wanted more room to expand. This was one of the chief reasons that it started war against the Philippines and other countries in the Far East. Another reason was that it wanted more products and these could be obtained only from other parts of the world.

For centuries before the war started, Japan had been ruled by a few rich and powerful families. These families owned most of the land, factories, mines, and other wealth in the country. The men in these families were well educated and many became generals, admirals, and other officers in the army and navy.

The rest of the Japanese people were extremely poor. Most of them had to work for the rich families and had no land of their own. They had no right to help choose the officials who ran the government. Many of them knew how to read and write, but few had attended college.

Through the years the poor people of Japan had become tired of war. Fathers and sons had been gone for long periods of time, and workers had been taxed heavily to carry on the war. Now the soldiers were coming home, wounded, ragged, and ill. Many longed for a new government, like the one in the United States.

General MacArthur helped the country to obtain a new government. He led the people to adopt a new constitution much like the Constitution of the United States. Under this constitution the people were allowed to elect their own representatives. Even women, who never had many rights in Japan, were allowed to vote. Now with a new government, the country never could be governed by a few rich families again.

The land which had belonged to the rich families was to be broken up into small tracts and sold to the poor people. This act made it possible for many Japanese farmers to own land of their own for the first time. They were far more contented to cultivate their own land instead of working for someone else.

Laws were passed limiting the number of hours persons could be required to work in factories, and improving the working conditions for women. Previously people had been required to work many hours a day at low wages, and women had earned about half as much as men.

Many changes were made in the schools. All children were required to attend school until they were fifteen. More young persons were encouraged to attend colleges and universities, including girls, who had not been admitted before. Special new courses were set up to train scientists and to help other workers prepare for the future. New textbooks were written.

The United States government helped the Japanese to build and equip modern factories. It sent many experts to help plan the factories and to find markets for Japanese goods in other parts of the world.

The Japanese people became happy and contented under the new form of government. They elected their own representatives to run the government. They worked shorter hours, but had more money than they had ever had before. They had more freedom in every day living. Their children obtained more education.

As time went on, the people developed great respect for MacArthur. He had reformed and improved their country beyond anything they had expected. He had not punished them for waging a war against his own country. Finally they came to cheer him wherever he went.

Another Task
for the General

By 1950 Japan, under General MacArthur's command, was well on the way to recovery from the war. The former enemy country had now become a close friend of the United States. The Japanese people looked to our country for guidance and felt grateful for our help.

By now fighting had broken out in northern Korea, an ancient country in Asia which borders China and Russia. This country forms a peninsula which juts into the ocean only a short distance from Japan. Following the war it had been ruled by the United Nations, but now was being invaded by troops from North Korea.

188

General MacArthur, at his headquarters in Japan, soon heard of the fighting. "General," he was told by members of his staff, "we have just received word that troops in North Korea have attacked South Korea."

President Truman recommended that General MacArthur be put in charge of the United Nations forces in Korea. These forces were made up of troops from many countries, who spoke differently, dressed differently, and fought differently. They were hard to combine into a single fighting army.

The President placed all the air, navy, and ground forces under General MacArthur's control. The President wanted MacArthur's military forces to be as powerful as possible.

When MacArthur reached Korea, he drove over much of the territory he would have to defend. He wanted to see what the country was like so that he could plan his strategy. For a

189

while the North Korean invasions were successful. More and more land was conquered.

Finally General MacArthur was able to organize his own fighting forces, and gradually won back much of the land which the invaders had taken. Some of his battles resulted in taking thousands of prisoners.

In time the United States felt that the invaders had been pushed back far enough and called MacArthur home. "Jeannie," he said to his wife, "we're going home at last."

The Japanese greatly mourned his departure from their part of the world. When he reached the United States, he received a hero's welcome in every city he passed through, from San Francisco to Cleveland, to New York.

In a speech to Congress, he said, "I am closing 52 years of military service. . . . an old soldier who tried to do his duty as God gave him the light to see that duty. Good by."

In 1962 when MacArthur was 82 years old, he was asked to review and address the cadets at West Point. "Beautiful place, West Point," said the doorman as MacArthur left his hotel for the academy. "Have you been there?"

In his speech to the cadets, the general said, "Duty-Honor-Country. Those three hallowed words dictate what you ought to be, what you can be, and what you will be. . . .

"I want you to know that when I cross the river my last conscious thought will be The Corps-and The Corps-and The Corps."

About two years later, the great general died in Washington, D. C. He was given a state funeral for his many services to his country. West Point cadets marched in his honor.

One of the greatest military leaders of his times had fought his last battle. The man who had been called "the bravest man in the world" was dead. And the country he had believed worth fighting for and worth dying for was the poorer by his passing.

More About This Book

WHEN DOUGLAS MACARTHUR LIVED

1880   DOUGLAS MACARTHUR WAS BORN, JANUARY 26.

There were thirty-eight states in the Union.

Rutherford B. Hayes was President.

The population of the country was about 50,155,000.

1880–
1899   DOUGIE LIVED WITH HIS PARENTS AT SEVERAL ARMY POSTS IN THE UNITED STATES.

The first electric street railway in the U.S. was operated in Baltimore, 1885.

The American Federation of Labor was organized, 1886.

Henry Ford built his first gas engine, 1893, and his first automobile, 1896.

1899–
1918   MACARTHUR STARTED A MILITARY CAREER AND FOUGHT IN WORLD WAR I.

Wilbur and Orville Wright flew the first heavier-than-air aircraft, 1903.

Robert Peary discovered the North Pole, 1909.

The United States entered World War I, 1917.

1918– MACARTHUR CONTINUED HIS MILITARY CAREER
1941 AND TRAINED THE PHILIPPINE ARMY.

The League of Nations was founded, 1920.

Stock market prices crashed and a severe depression followed, 1929.

World War II began in Europe, 1939.

1941– MACARTHUR FOUGHT IN WORLD WAR II, OCCU-
1951 PIED JAPAN, AND DIRECTED FORCES IN KOREA.

The United States entered World War II, following an attack by Japan, 1941.

The United Nations Charter was adopted, establishing a world organization, 1945.

The North Atlantic Treaty Organization was established, 1949.

1951– MACARTHUR LIVED IN RETIREMENT AND
1964 SERVED AS A BUSINESS EXECUTIVE.

Nautilus, first atomic-powered submarine, was launched, 1954.

Alaska and Hawaii became the forty-ninth and fiftieth states, 1959.

Three United States manned flights into orbit took place, 1962.

194

1964 DOUGLAS MACARTHUR DIED IN WASHINGTON, D.C., APRIL 5.

There were fifty states in the Union.

Lyndon B. Johnson was President.

The population of the United States was about 191,325,000.

DO YOU REMEMBER?

1. Why did the soldiers at Fort Wingate have trouble with the Navaho Indians?

2. What great sorrow came to the MacArthur family while they lived in New Mexico?

3. How did Arthur and Dougie get into trouble for playing with the heliograph?

4. How did Dougie win appointment to the United States Military Academy at West Point?

5. How did young MacArthur suffer from hazing during his first year at West Point?

6. How did MacArthur have an opportunity to visit Japan and other countries of Asia?

7. How did MacArthur win honors for leading his troops in World War I?

195

8. How did MacArthur drive the bonus marchers from Washington, D.C.?

9. What did MacArthur and President Quezon discover on their journey together?

10. How did MacArthur attempt to defend the Philippines from the Japanese?

11. What did MacArthur mean by saying "I shall return," when leaving Corregidor?

12. How did MacArthur manage to recapture the Philippines?

13. How did MacArthur demonstrate great leadership in dealing with Japan?

14. How did MacArthur help to save South Korea from communist aggression?

IT'S FUN TO LOOK UP THESE THINGS

1. How are young men selected today for the U.S. Military Academy at West Point?

2. What are the four most important branches of the armed services?

3. Why is it necessary for the United States to maintain a large army today?

196

4. What steps must a young man take to enlist in the United States Army?

5. Who is the present Chief of Staff of the United States Army?

6. Why is it important to have Japan and the Philippines as friends in the Pacific?

7. What rank in the United States Army did MacArthur hold at the time of his death?

INTERESTING THINGS YOU CAN DO

1. Explain what takes place at an army base where soldiers are stationed.

2. Make a list of different official ranks that MacArthur held in the army.

3. Draw a map to show different places where MacArthur fought in World War II.

4. Collect photographs of MacArthur for a display on the bulletin board.

5. Prepare a chart, showing important assignments MacArthur carried on in the army.

6. Read more about General Jonathan Wainwright, and give a report to the class.

OTHER BOOKS YOU MAY ENJOY READING

Army Times. Famous Military Leaders of World War II, Editors of Army Times. Dodd-Mead.

Franklin Roosevelt: Boy of the Four Freedoms, Ann Weil. Trade and School Editions, Bobbs-Merrill.

Picture Story of the Philippines, Hester O'Neill. McKay.

Story of World War II, The, Robert Leckie. Random House.

Visit with Us in Japan, Joan Pross Larson. Prentice-Hall.

West Point Story, Nardi R. Campion and Red Reeder. Random House.

INTERESTING WORDS IN THIS BOOK

adequate (ăd'ē̇ kwĭt) : enough, as much as needed

assassinate (ă̇ săs'ĭ nāt) : murder by surprise or treacherous tactics

butte (būt) : steep hill, standing alone

cache (kăsh) : hiding place used for storing provisions or implements

century (sĕn'tu̇ rĭ) : one hundred years

ceremony (sĕr'ĕ mō'nĭ) : planned program of events taking place, as for graduation

consequence (kŏn'sĕ kwĕns) : result

constitution (kŏn'stĭ tū'shŭn) : document stating or outlining principles of government

corps (kōrz) : large military unit

Corregidor (kŏ rĕg'ĭ dôr) : island fort at entrance of Manila Bay in the Philippine Islands

defiance (dĕ fī'ănce) : act of ignoring or opposing something, as a command

enthusiasm (ĕn thū'zĭ ăz'm) : zeal

especially (ĕs pĕsh'ăl ĭ) : particularly, chiefly

haze (hāz) : harass with ridiculous tasks

heliograph (hē'lĭ ŏ grȧf') : apparatus for signalling by means of sunlight thrown from a mirror

Hiroshima (hē'rȯ shē'mȧ) : city in Japan where first atomic bomb was dropped

interpreter (ĭn tûr'prĕt ēr) : person who translates orally from one language to another

investigate (ĭn vĕs tĭ gāt) : study carefully, examine closely

Leyte (lā'tĕ) : island in the Pacific Ocean, one of the Philippines

Luzon (lōō zŏn') : largest and most important island in the Philippines

miracle (mĭr'ȧ k'l) : unusual happening beyond the known laws of nature

monotonous (mỏ nŏt'ỏ nŭs) : uniform and uninteresting

Nagasaki (nä'gȧ sä'kė) : city in Japan where second atomic bomb was dropped

peninsula (pĕn ĭn'sû lȧ) : large area of land extending into water

plantation (plăn tā'shŭn) : large tract of land cultivated by laborers

pneumonia (nů mō'nĭ ȧ) : disease caused by inflammation of the lungs

Quezon, Manuel (kā'sôn) : first president of the Philippine Commonwealth

specialist (spĕsh'ăl ĭst) : person who devotes himself to certain specific work

strategy (străt'e jĭ) : act of planning and directing military operations

strenuous (strĕn'ů ŭs) : extremely hard

surrender (sŭ rĕn'dēr) : give up

Tokyo (tō'kĭ ō) : capital of Japan and the largest city in the world

treason (trē'z'n) : act of betraying or helping to overthrow one's own country